A COOT COMES CLEAN

A COOT COMES CLEAN

VOLUME I OF THE MOTORCYCLE CHRONICLES CONTAINING SEVEN TALES FROM A COLD WAR SURVIVIOR.

SELECTED FROM THE WRYDER COLLECTIVE.

ROBERT BUSSARD

GCP

All stories contained in this volume are based on memories of The Wryder Collective which have been fictionalized by the author. Characters belonging to the collective are identified as such. Any resemblance of other characters to actual persons is coincidental. Descriptions of events should not be interpreted as fully accurate historical accounts.

Opinions expressed in the narrative may or may not be those currently held by the author. They are contextual with the period of the story in which they are expressed or are summations of thoughts expressed to the author by other persons or entities.

ISBN: 978-1978228818

Dedicated to Otho

TABLE OF CONTENTS

PREFACE

Preface

The stories contained in this book are all true, more or less. Frighteningly more than less according to Wryder. **Wryder is the passive narrator, chief protagonist and proprietor of the set from which these yarns have been selected. He refers to this set of tales as The Motorcycle Chronicles or MC.** Only occasionally and incidentally do they have anything directly to do with motorcycles, but motorcycles are one of the longest running matter strings in the collective. This first volume of MC contains seven tales; they were not chosen chronologically; however, they are all from the earlier years of Wryder's animation.

In addition to MC **there is another set to be noted and that is The Wryder Collective, WC.** Among other "wanna' be" pursuits, Wryder is a ne'r do well mathematician and has organized his existence using set theory.

> *A set is a collection of "things" (objects, numbers…characters, etc.).*
>
> *Each member of the set is called an element of the set.*
>
> *All members are unique, there is only one of each.*

WC is a set containing a variety of elements: some emotions, extraneous thoughts, a few instincts, various smells and a handful of anthropomorphized motorcycles as well as other vehicles. However, most of the things in WC are character elements.

These elements provide the chronicles' narrative. They are the substrate components of the Wryder persona. Wryder has experienced his existence through them, often with one being predominant, but as a permutation of all of them. Each has their own compartment or experience specialty, but they are never isolated from one another and Wryder sits as the final arbiter of who does what and who lives the lion's share of each chronicle.

Thinking of Wryder and WC as the same entity will not lend confusion to any of the stories. However, there is one important distinction to be clear about should one choose to quantify his/her life using set theory or a similar model.

WC "is", it exists digitally, temporarily static on ever ascending planes of definition. Not all elements of WC are yet discovered, be they character elements or otherwise. Like the long-predicted Higgs Boson whose actual discovery and verification of existence took decades and development of the Hadron Supercollider. There must exist yet undiscovered elements of WC which account for its ability to interact with the entirety of its realm in the manner as it has been observed to do. When elemental discoveries are made, WC's configuration is then redefined, but between those discoveries it is statically quantifiable. It is knowable.

On the other hand, Wryder "is becoming". His maturation is dynamic, progressing along an analogical and asymptotic trajectory towards self- actualization. There are no naturally occurring planes of animation or realm interaction plateaus. Observationally, one can pick a moment and say that Wryder is this or is that. But, that observation is obsolete instantaneously with its selection. One cannot comprehend what "is" before it becomes what "was". Therefore, no description of Wryder's state can ever be fully current. Nor can it be fully accurate due to the *Observer Effect which states that simply observing a situation or phenomenon necessarily changes that phenomenon.* Unlike WC, Wryder is not knowable, but he is learnable.

As previously stated, the difference does not affect interpretation of the following chronicles. Also, note that the tone of the chronicles is generally more guttural and visceral than has been the language of this brief explanation of WC, MC and Wryder. This is largely due to the period, situations and elements these chronicles were drawn from.

Chapter 1 Crab

A Motorcycle Chronicle from the Wryder Collective Featuring Service (circa 1979). Dream input by Driver (an adolescent element of WC).

In this story Service is the 21-year-old, military substrate element of Wryder. If Service were discovered today, he likely would be called Warrior as that term is more in vogue these days. Service suits him better, because it is what he provided. He is a Cold War veteran and survivor and lends this essence to the whole of WC.

Driver, car-owning adolescent of WC, once described to me a recurring dream he frequently had as a young man. However, WC's last remembered occurrence of the dream for many, many years was by Service, WC's military persona. The dream had some sexual aspects to it and the reason for its latent reanimation by Service will become clear, shortly. The occasion was during the second week of Service's basic training. In confirming that his version of the dream was the same as Driver had described to me, Service mentioned to me another event that he recalled near the end of his basic training. An event to be described to you now.

Sharing a room with fifty other young men tends to inhibit that most important, oft performed and somber ritual known as masturbation, unless of course you are from

Mississippi. In that case the word "inhibition" has no known definition. These fellows were easy to identify, especially at night. Just listen for the loudest squeaking set of bedsprings and you could be pretty sure it was occupied by one of them sweet rebel boys. One such Neanderthal-haired specimen named Johnny was the first Mississippi resident Service ever met. He was also the first -person Service ever heard utter the phrase, "I'd eat a yard of her shit just to see where it come from." This was in reference to his sweet and apparently quite dear sister-in-law. So much for Philadelphia as the city of brotherly love, Jackson, Mississippi perhaps.

The one and only town pass, the sole time Service and his many roommates were allowed to leave the base during basic training came on Saturday of the seventh week. While Service and most of his flight[1] mates were taking in the highly anti-climactic Alamo in downtown San Antonio, Johnny was making good on his declaration vis-à-vis his sister-in-law.

The next night following the return from town pass began normally, but after lights out it seemed there was more bedsprings action than typical. Admittedly after seven weeks, inhibitions were down and wet dreams thought dormant sense puberty, if there is such a thing as an end

---

[1] A flight is like a platoon.

to male puberty, had been reanimated. Such had been the case for Service as evidenced by his appropriation of Driver's dream.

It was still reasonably quiet, but steadily becoming noisier as the sound from the squeaking springs was now augmented by a rhythmic and steadily intensifying scratching noise. Not exactly like steel brushes on a snare drum skin, something more like the sound of steel wool rubbed on a rusty bucket, but with a fleshier resonance.

Suddenly, the "squeak, scratch, squeak, but otherwise quiet" darkness was pierced by an unmanly, high-pitched shriek. "Crabs! I got fucking crabs!" echoed through the instantaneously frozen barracks. 20 to 30 seconds of stunned silence followed before giving way to a symphony of disgusted recriminations. Fuck! Oh Fuck! Son of a bitch! Me too! Jesus Christ on a bike! Fuck! This continued for some time. Only Service and about five others remained silent, their hands not jerking back and forth in their underwear. Service wanted to scratch too, but he told himself it was psychosomatic and after 5 minutes of forcing his hands to remain still and out of his underwear, he convinced himself he was right. Indeed, his itch ceased, but would flare again briefly several times during the next couple of days.

1-3

Crab

Immediately upon the heels of the horrendous discovery and shocked exclamations, the accusations begin to fly. As in all problem situations, the placing of blame is the most important item early in the resolution process. It is so important that in some groups, before anything even goes awry they designate a scapegoat so that blame is already automatically set even before the disaster falls. This is a good way to jumpstart the resolution process, but the young men were not yet that experienced at problem solving.

.

As noted, all the young men save five or six were scratching, but obviously there was no way 95% of them in this room had gotten laid during town pass. 1 or 2% tops, besides even if they all had partaken of Texas hospitality there was no way each of them was now incubating vermin. This was not like in the movie *Biloxi Blues,* they could not all have gone to the same woman. Time alone would not have permitted that. Also making it statistically impossible, was the fact that none of them stayed in groups of more than two or three after getting off the bus from base.

Under examination by a spontaneously organized kangaroo court, an effort was initiated to determine who all had gotten pussy on town pass. Christ the whole fucking city of San Antonio couldn't be infested! The

1-4

Crab

entire God Damn town would need to go under quarantine if that many of them had picked up crabs during a six-hour pass! The examination stagnated in a dilemma. People were lying. They eventually figured out who, but it would have been immediately obvious to more experienced and cleverer thinking men.

Young men lie about their sexual exploits. The majority of boys in Service's flight claimed to have gotten laid during town pass. It was what you did if you had your shit together. Most of the liars held out under cross examination for a minute or two, but caved when the accusation of having been the one who had borne crabs to his 50+ roommates begin to fall upon them. It was one thing to have gone sexless and have to own up to it, however this was not as difficult a cross to bear as that of being "the carrier".

So, it finally came down to only two self-professed practitioners of poon. One skinny kid clung to his story, claiming he had even gotten it for free, because he was so charming. That was his give away, one look at him and you could tell he was just another poor, limp dick bastard like the rest of them. Besides, he was from California, it wasn't a given that pussy was even his bag.
Ultimately, it boiled down to Johnny from Mississippi, that yard o' shit eatin' motherfucker. Well, not really, it

1-5

Crab

wasn't his mother, some surprise there, but his charming sister-in-law of whom he had spoken so eloquently and enchantingly. She had come down to visit him and in brotherly (in-law) fashion, for Mississippi, Service guessed, he'd fucked her.

Apparently, she had several other brother-in- laws or Johnny's brother got around, but somebody in the family tree was spreading around more than the clan newsletter.

Having boiled it down to the actual guilty party, one would have expected the angry villagers to then turn on the itching monster with torches and pitch forks. Not so, learned Service that night. It's not what crime you do that merits what justice you receive, it simply comes down to who is on the jury.

Johnny was likable enough and not without a certain rustic and charismatic charm unique to the inbred. He always made you feel like family or at least that he was willing to treat you as such. Of course, being "family" in that clan garnered you relations with a few more privileges than most of us are accustomed to. He made the wise play, no attempt to deny. He ran headlong into the accusations. Hell yeah, he'd fucked his sister-in-law, told all about it right down to that first yard he'd had to digest. He related and embellished with such gusto that

1-6

Crab

within a few minutes he had the flight eating out of his hand, salivating for each juicy detail of the blow-by-blow action. It isn't a new phenomenon, most of our heroes have always been cheap.

About this time the barracks bay door slammed open and a Smokey Bear hat stormed in with one pissed off drill instructor underneath it. The DI had been sleeping at home, a luxury not afforded him in the earlier weeks of basic training, when he got the call. He had slept in his office in the early weeks to ensure there was no after lights out activity. In other words, the kind of crap that was going on right now. There was no facetiously pleasant greeting, such as, "good morning, ladies". It was right down to cases. "What in the name of Jesus H. Fucking Christ is going on here!?" was the first thing Service heard him say, but by no means the last.

Sovereignty and jurisdiction of the kangaroo court dissolved instantly as jurisprudence past to a higher authority, to the drill instructor, or God of all Airmen Basics. GAB, as Service will refer to him from here on. Service and the rest of the quivering piss ants were all Airmen Basics or ABs (the lowest rank possible). To say GAB ruled with an iron hand would be to overstate the strength of iron. His bale was a little further up the periodic chart of elements than the mere ferrous metals, perhaps even being some sort of titanium molecular alloy. The Inquisition began. However, GAB did not actually wait for answers to any of the questions that he was firing off with machine gun like syncopation.

The answers wouldn't have mattered anyway, as the questions were more rhetorical, in fact downright accusatorial. Hell, they were all guilty from the moment his home phone had rang, anyhow. There was so much choice narrative spewing forth from GAB that Service could not take it all in, so cannot now remember it verbatim. He does recall the gist of it and knew even at the time that he was in the presence of a linguistic artist. Say what you will about the one-sidedness of his communication style, the man nonetheless had an impressive lexicon. But, GAB also had an overactive sense of entitlement, causing him to come off as being very possessive.

"You dirty, filthy, pecker in pussy dippin' sons of bitches, you snatch snot gobblin' bastards! How dare you bring crabs into MY barracks!? I issued you pants from MY own store, money out of MY pocket, MY own pants with buttons on the fly. In those days ABs were not trusted with the use of zippers. I expected those buttons to be used! No one gave you permission to undo those buttons. Those buttons were there to protect you and your

1-8

Crab

worthless tally whackers. They were meant to keep healthy vermin like you in and crabs out of MY bedroom!"

There was that over possessive nature of his. His bedroom! The ABs slept there and cleaned it, but not like they we're about to do in the next couple of days. His referendum on personal reflection in which he forced them to look at themselves in light of various social mores, academic questions and an array of philosophical points of views continued thusly for about 45 minutes: By what right do any of you slug shit swallowin' scum dare to think any of you deserve pussy? How dare you despoil the very garments I have given you and the bodies I have built for you? If God, in this case himself, had intended for your puny penises to ever see the light of day, he (again himself) would have put them on your faces instead of hiding them between your legs where they're gonna' stay from this moment on, unless I stick them up your own asses. The rant finally ceased with an order.

"Drop your pants you infested hogs! Strip! Everybody put your shit in one pile right here! Get those socks off, I said naked!"

Unclad, the flight was now ordered to attention and directed to form a single line, penis towards the buttocks of the man in front of you, tighten up that line, space forward and face the shower. "I said, tighten up vermin harborers!" GAB snarled. "Now march your pestilence ridden asses into that shower and start scrubbing! Make that water hot and scrub like you're peelin' paint from a pew. I wanna' see steam in the air and flakes of skin on the floor!"

Service recalls, he was pretty much in the middle of this herd of fifty some young men in an area with five showerheads and enough room to reasonably accommodate five more standing and waiting their turn under the water. It was crowded. The sweat cloud from the body heat and fear alone would have produced the steamy haze GAB was looking for. Nevertheless, he insured the faucets were set to just 2° below scald. There was considerable milling about, as each AB jockeyed for a douse under the shower, at least enough to soak their hair as evidence they had obeyed GAB's command. After the first five no one went for the soap either, as it was now suspect for having already been touched by one of the "unclean".

"That was the slapstick hilarious part of the whole scene. Not at the time, but in a looking back at it years later sort of way", Service declared. The bodies were moving, seeking water, but oh so carefully. Each AB had their stomachs sucked in and were on their toes in an effort to displace their volume in a vertical rather than a horizontal direction. They moved sideways past each other, never allowing themselves to become trapped between two other moving bodies whose unexpected change of direction might squeeze them in the middle, causing both sides to come in contact with two other un-cleans at the same time. Moreover, frontal or rear contact had to be avoided at all cost. If someone, something, anything touched your anus, there was no telling what would happen. The delicate détente insured by the prospect of mutual humiliation may have been broken and a naked fracas of 50 men and God only knows how many bugs could breakout. Nothing but losers in that doomsday scenario. They moved carefully and continued to baste with GAB watching their every move. All the while, harboring the thought that they either had crabs or were about to contract them from their fellow constricts with the mortifying possibility that crabs might already be setting up a colony in the hair around their ass holes. "Daunting stuff", Service recalled understatedly.

Everyone wanted to get to the water, but by this late point in basic training, they all knew that no one wanted to be among the first out of the shower. It was axiomatic to GAB that if you were the first one to complete a task, any task, then you had not done a good enough job of it. First out, would be first sent right back in do it again. This

1-11

Crab

time you'd be starting at the back of the pack of slowly and carefully milling, nude infestees.

The situation was problematic as GAB continued to scream for the unclean masses to scrub and move their asses. A few of the unclad, quavering, wet young men lingered at the shower exit wishing they had not been so eager to get to the front of the water line. The exact physical laws that were at work at this moment, Service has never been able to positively explain. He believes it may have been a heretofore undiscovered law of physics overlooked by Newton, Einstein, and Hawking. It may be something he should name and put into the form of an equation. Sure, $e = mc^2$, or something like that. He could state it as a law maybe: a body in motion tends to stay in motion unless it encounters an equal and opposite force to that of its own momentum, everyone knows that. Service's equation of basic training might look something like this: AB times the fear of GAB squared is equal to the product of constipation factorialized times nervous paralysis.

To put it algebraically: $(AB) \times (FGAB)^2 = (C!) \times (NP)$. To reiterate, because this is important: Airman Basic times (Fear of GAB times Fear of GAB) is equal to, or equivalent with the product of

1-12

Crab

*Constipation Factorialized {i.e. C X [C-1] X [C-2] X …
X [(C+1)-C] times nervous paralysis.*

"Okay, okay, knock off the phony mathematical junk Service, just tell us what happened next without all the pseudoscientific crapola", I told Service.

"Well" he considered, "one of the unique properties of this law is that it can induce motion in a stationary mass, merely by proximity. That is, without the requirement of opposite magnetic force or reversed electrical polarity."
As near as Service has been able to determine; the following is how it applied on what has subsequently, at least as of this very second anyway, come to be known as *The Night of the Living Crab"*.

> *When a fear-paralyzed or otherwise static body is encroached upon another, known to be vermin infested body to within a distance from which the stationary body believes the vermin from the body in motion could make the leap across the space between them, the stationary body will assume motion in a direction opposite to and with momentum equal to or greater than that of the encroaching body.*

After a deep and discerning look of consternation from me, Service finally said, "okay, let me put it into layman's terms as many of the young men were able to do in that long-ago shower."

"Back off, you bastard! Don't fucking touch me!"

 To GAB's continuous lament of what a filthy, worthless bunch of slobs he had been given to try and mold into functional, albeit still maggot like men, the flight of naked bodies was eventually herded through the shower and back into a line. They toweled off, though it was somewhat pointless due to the steamy clouds still hanging in the air and were marched back into the sleeping bay. Service was thinking the whole time that this was one fucking bizarre and unique event he was caught up in. However, GAB's tone sounded well practiced. Sure, he was screaming, but by now Service knew that was just part of the ambience of basic training. Service pondered, "How many times had he done this before?" GAB was using specific adjectives, ones that went right to the heart of the crab matter. These could not be right off the top of his head. He'd have to be Mickey Spillane to come up with some of this shit that quickly. Was this whole crab shower just another of the common rituals?" Service would never know for sure, but fortunately it remained unique for him. He has to date

1-14

Crab

never again showered with 50 other crab bearing men, not knowingly anyhow.

Just as he was about to move on with this story, picking it up back in the sleeping bay, Service remembered another small, tangent event that took place before the march began.

There was a minor delay before the naked march back to the bunks began, where levels of degradation the likes of which Service had never previously imagined would ensue. One stupid bastard, one unadulterated, Ohioan undoubtedly, nincompoop decided that since he was already in the latrine and felt the urge he would go ahead, step out of line over to the urinal and pee. You know, to save having to get back up later. The rest of the line stood horrified as this fucking moron broke ranks to relieve himself. Service realized this could not end well, though to be fair the kid was probably so nervous he would have pissed himself in line if he hadn't made the dash. In true *Kobayashi Maru* fashion, it was a no-win scenario for him.

The number of GAB's laws the Ohioan imbecile had broken was considerable: right off the bat he had made a decision, this was not within the purview of an AB. GAB was doing the thinking and deciding for them. He had not confirmed with GAB that his need to urinate was genuine and not just some sophomoric attempt to get out of an unpleasant detail as the history of GAB's decisions proved that it almost always was. He had walked barefoot to within range of the urinal, something forbidden to prevent spread of disease. It was a little late to worry about what might be spread, besides as Service knew from personal effort these latrine floors were so clean the Holy Virgin Mary herself would be pleased to eat off them. There were many other misdemeanor offenses committed by the Ohioan AB, too many for Service to remember, but he does recall that GAB's admonitions with extreme emphasis only ended after finally haranguing the AB for having in his nervous haste and ill-conceived act of wanton bladder easement, aimed poorly and moistened GAB's urinal cake. Yeah, that damn GAB sure figured he owned everything.

The offending AB finally rejoined the line, quickly catching a drop of pee posed on the tip of his penis before it dripped to the floor whereby another lengthy diatribe would have ensued regarding the lack of respect being shown to "GAB's" floor.

The march back to the sleeping bay was relatively calm with no abrupt halts and no buttocks/penis contact, a profound fear of the young men at this moment. All the ABs now stood at attention, including one kid from Idaho who had a nervous induced boner. To the grace of God (the actual one) goes the credit for GAB not having noticed this. Service did not know what such an infraction would be called, but he was positive that a boner in naked formation would call for more hideous retribution then your common misdemeanor type screw up. It would undoubtedly be worse than the tongue lashing received for moistening GAB's urinal cake. Who knew the penalty for offending GAB's solemn dignity?

So, it looked like the initial phase of the crab ordeal was almost over. They would be told to get their crab harboring asses in bed and go to sleep. The order came, "strip 'em!"

"Strip what? I'm already naked!" wondered Service for an instant. Then he glanced down at the bed, more of a cot with springs and a mattress really. He looked at those four tight, perfect hospital corners and thought, "man, what a waste!" If one slept carefully, didn't move around or rollover and slid into the bed from the pillow end without throwing back the blanket and sheet, at least two and sometimes three of those meticulously shaped corners could be preserved. In the morning all you had to do was a little yank for tightening that last corner, then you were good to go. Besides the time management aspect of this approach, it also had a beneficial effect on quality control.

The corners looked the same, every morning, because they were the same. This desire for standardization was another characteristic of GAB's that affected him almost as acutely as the possessiveness. This second obsession of his was also precisely why you never wore a clean pair of underwear from your drawer once it had been folded so that it measured from 6.000 to 6.250 inches across the waistband and was placed no closer than 3.125 inches to 3.250 inches from the T-shirts which were bent, starched heavier than a fat kid on an all potato salad diet and located with similar levels of tolerance in your foot locker.

Screw that! Now, he'd be starting from scratch. But, Service accepted the inevitable and began tearing the linen from his bunk. As with the clothes earlier, everything went into one large pile which would soon be hauled off by the two hapless lottery winners that happened to be on laundry detail that night.

Clean blankets, pillowcases and sheets were doled out. The bed making began with everyone aware that even if you got those corners so tight your ass would bounce right off if you tried to sit on the bed, which of course you were never allowed to do, each bed would be made, torn back apart by GAB and remade at least twice. It was the first out of the shower thing all over again. The thing was to hold back on finishing. Not so much that you were caught malingering, but until GAB had torn apart enough beds that he might forget that yours hadn't been one of them yet.

It can be accomplished as a solitary task, but a truly tight, bounce a quarter on it, taught as a trampoline made bed with hospital corners on it so close to exactly 55° angles that neither Euclid or Pythagoras themselves could have proven otherwise, well, this a two-person operation. Service and the guy in the bunk next to him first made Service's bed and then that of the other still naked AB. With one guy on each side of the bed and each pulling as hard as they could, it was possible to really ratchet up the tension, so the linen stretched tighter than the skin on Mary Tyler Moore's face after a "procedure". The two ABs got both bunks made up while only having to redo one of them a second time; it having failed the obviously subjective scrutiny of GAB.

It was getting late in the night or early in the morning Service supposed. A sense of urgency saturated the air propagated by GAB's only barely beginning to subside furor. Service was trying to convince himself that the flight was now coming to the trailing edge of the storm. There had been no relatively calm eye as supposedly storms have. Or else, the naked ABs had skirted around that hoped-for respite, instead remaining ensconced in an active portion of the tempest for its full duration. Whether the storm was ebbing or not, one dark cloud still floated on Service's horizon.

He was concerned about the continued nakedness. It was not in the ABs' best interest to remain unclad. Most of them were still scratching to relieve an either real or imaginary itch and they needed at least a thin layer of protective cotton between their fingernails and their more tender hair zones. Normally, for the bizarro world that is basic training anything the ABs thought good for themselves, having underwear on for example, GAB thought of as not so good. Particularly, if it served to foster any shred of rapidly becoming extinct dignity that some of these obstinate bastard ABs were clinging to like dung balls on a hairy ass.

In this singular case however, Service could not understand how their balls hanging out was in any way advantageous to GAB. He had very strongly in the past and of course, again just this night, reiterated repeatedly how utterly worthless, disgusting and vile those crab infested genitals and tangent regions were to him. It was therefore inconceivable to Service why they had not been ordered to cover their offending areas. GAB certainly did not display any affectations suggesting that he might be enjoying the naked revelry. The ass crack exposure alone

1-20

Crab

during the bed making frenzy would have turned the stomachs of lesser desensitized men. Yeah, that seed of doubt that there still wasn't more humiliation, another slap of indignity to the face yet to come, hung out there in Service's mind like one mighty big, freaking matzo ball.

GAB ordered them all to stand at attention at the foot of their bunks and had each row count off. The odd numbers were told to turn to their left, the even numbers to their right. Whoever they faced would be their still nude, hard-nippled and shrivel-penised partner for the next task. The evening was cool and their toweling off had been ineffective following the pore dilating, steam shower/scald and the moisture evaporating from their skin had been chilling. For those rows which did not have an even number of bunks and men, some miserable fuck next to last in the row would have first one partner and then another in the non-musically accompanied dance of the damned they were about to perform. Service has since come to refer to it as "*Beelzebub's Ball*!"

"Buddy check!" GAB bellowed. Service had an instant flashback to the memories of Pedaler from Junior Grange Camp. Pedaler is the ten-year-old persona of WC and one of Service's fellow elements in that set. The same command was given every few minutes and you had to quit swimming and look around to see if your appointed

"Buddy" had drowned yet or not. After everyone was seen holding someone else's hand in the air with their own it was okay to continue swimming, or trying to drown your buddy or peeing in the lake or whatever you had been doing.

None of the ABs were swimming. In fact, there wasn't even any water around. Why would they have to grasp and hold up the hand of another AB? There would be touching, but it would not be hand-to-hand. As it turned out, that form of combat would have been preferred to the kind of bodily contact they would be making.

GAB began to explain, "Alright now, each of you are gonna' check your buddy over for crabs, lice or any other filthy parasites you disgusting pigs are providing a home for! This ain't gonna' be no quick glance over, you're gonna' examine each other like you're performing an autopsy on a murder victim from the British Royal Fuckin' Family. You'll start at the scalp, running your fingers through your buddy's bristles, the predetermined hairstyle for basic training. Work your way down, check armpits, ear hair, nose hair, back hair, every one of his fuckin' follicles. Now when you get to the middle section, I wanna' see some serious scouting. If I come behind you and find one fuckin' flea that you missed, you'll be eating it. This is to be a tactile inspection gentleman (an ironic

1-22

Crab

description, Service thought there had been far too much touching already). When you get to a hairy patch, touch it. I wanna' see handfuls of those dead little bastards!"

The loudest silent groan Service never heard emanated from the bay. On the fortunate side, there was an even number of men in Service's row with him being the last AB, so only one buddy for him. On the other hand, Service's buddy was a Sasquatch from the Northwest named Uramaya Yeti. He had the hair of a low land gorilla. Service wondered if he might be a friend with Jane Goodall or Diane Fosse. Certainly, one or both of them had studied him.

A lot of men remember their first time having sex as being the end of their youthful innocence. The act of lovemaking for the first time as the embarkation point to becoming a different kind of man. Service had thought so too, but in the ensuing 10 minutes he was disenfranchised of that notion. It is usually not in the moment of it that one realizes the activity he is involved in is one of those "life-changing" kinds. An actualization of that depth and meaning is most often not understood until years of pondering and weighing of the events against all other aspects of one's experience has taken place. This freaky happenstance and its significance to Service's and later to WC's existence had no such subtlety. It crashed into his psyche with the force of a rogue sun gone supernova. No pondering required.

Taking on the affectations of a pride, herd, group, bunch, colony, whatever they're called, of pink ass baboons, ironically the AB's asses also had a crimson glow at that moment, the white boys anyway, the flight, pride, group ... whatever... began to groom each other. Service thought to himself, "wow, we're literally picking bugs off each other". Darwin was rolling over in his grave and in the backdrop of his brain, Service could hear the role of kettledrums and visualize himself grasping a large femur bone of some dead, decayed animal and brandishing it menacingly over his head as he was approached by threatening looking beings that were just a little bit different from him. Bigger, but not smarter. On second estimate, they'd have to be smarter. Look what he was doing, and he hadn't been drafted, he'd volunteered.

Service couldn't say that there wasn't a tinge of exhilaration from the pure primal notion of the event as he finger-combed his way through Uramaya's scalp before progressing, an odd term to use given his current direction of evolution, to Uri's carboniferous back hair. Someday Uri would be a noble silverback, leading his group through dense foliage to safety and a good food source. The majesty of his behavior would be captured in

1-24

Crab

an Oscar winning for best documentary film produced by National Geographic. Service would be able to say, "I knew him when..." he mused. They had been told by GAB that it would take about 10 minutes to adequately inspect their buddy.

Service calculated in his head. Christ! He wouldn't even be down to the pubic region in 10 minutes. Fuck, everyone would think he was intentionally lingering, perhaps relishing the opportunity. The detrimental potential of that aftermath, not to mention becoming the only one still looking, the only one for GAB to still be watching was not to be contemplated. So, he was panicked into a greater sense of urgency and an affinity for his task like Donald Trump to the Jackass Liar Hall of Fame. Wait! GAB would understand, he'd see that jungle and realize that Service was virtually looking for Dr. Livingston! Bullshit! GAB would not make allowances, there was nothing in the manual about the unfair nature of searching for crabs on a Sasquatch! Why would there be? How often did this come up? This might be the most unique male experience since the Neanderthals roamed Europe and one lucky, slope skulled, long eared bastard hooked up with a Cro-Magnon chick and initiated the proliferation of the Basque genome.

1-25

Crab

Service would just skip on down, act like he'd checked it all. What if he missed some, even one? This thought did not whet his appetite as he remembered GAB's imposition regarding the fortune of any missed crab and the inspector who had let it slip between his fingers. Oh! double fuck!

The pubic region, he'd have to get his fingers in there! Triple fuck! thought Service as an exaggerated escape of air from his lungs deflated him. His bile sac imploded in his stomach and he began to taste yesterday's asparagus. Shit? Uramaya Yeti's pea patch waited down there for him. It did not beckon him like an adventure through the Amazonian jungle, equipped with guides and porters. His anticipation was of a more threatening nature, more ominous. He would be on a sojourn through an equatorial hell of dense, damp Brillo pad foliage with carnivorous beast of prey stalking him, hidden behind every metallic bristle.

Then he was there at the precipice of the pubic escarpment. GAB was on him now too, right behind him, examining, measuring his dedication and effectiveness for the task at hand. His hands, he would have to move them now. Maybe it was good that GAB was menacing him. This way he could not delay, could not stop it, would not have to think about it.

1-26

Crab

"Catch any yet AB?" GAB queried.

"Sir, no sir", stammered Service in the approved AB response lexicon.

"Well, get your fingers in there! They are not gonna' start waving white flags and yellin' we give up, we give up at ya'! Dig, dammit dig!"

"Sir, yes, sir", issued from Service reflexively. He thought about closing his eyes, but didn't. He had to know how close his hands were to "it". GAB moved on to the next row of beds as Uramaya's lance like bristles began to sting Service's fingers and puncture his soul.

You know how sometimes you have a tremendous dread of something and then it turns out not to be that bad after all. This was not one of those times, Service assured me. It was worse than he ever imagined it could be.

Each irregularity discovered by his probing fingers had to be inspected, identified, and appraised. Now crabs are small, one must get uncomfortably close to determine the nature of any object that size. As it happened, there were plenty of objects unearthed, or un-pubed, as it were, requiring forensic examination. However, each

Crab

turned out to be merely a broken loose scab, a detached piece of Brillo pad, a soiled piece of underwear lint, or an unidentifiable tiny yellow, crystalline substance, or other relatively inoffensive specimen of matter.

He could do it, Service could get through this. 50 other guys were doing it. Ah yes, there it is, the salvationary notion of mankind. 50 other guys are doing it! As a kid, when your mother asks you if you'd jump off a bridge just because "50 other boys were doing it", you'd respond no. But, the answer in your head was yes, Fuck yeah you would do it! One of the few fates worse than dying from jumping off a bridge was to be caught not doing what all of your friends, or enemies for that matter, were doing. You'd jump from that bridge in a heartbeat with an ear to ear, shit eating grin on your fucking face to prove that a 50-foot plunge to a boulder strewn piss puddle of water was no big deal. Fuckin' 'ay, misery loves company! Who do you think built them God damn pyramids or that Great Wall of China? It wasn't one guy without a mother. This is the postulate that makes basic training work. We're all gonna' do it! It is at the heart of men's survival, not women's, just men's survival.

Okay thought Service, he wasn't the only poor bastard crab fishin' from this morally leaky boat. Of course, the other 49 dignity stripped devils weren't follicle fingering their way around a motherfuckin' abominable snowman. One lucky son of a bitch had drawn a buddy who had that weird condition where they cannot grow any body hair at all. It'd be worth the risk of getting caught to steal any lottery ticket that dude ever bought.

"Moses on a pogo stick!" squealed Service's brain, look at Uramaya's balls! They were like a pair of supermarket coconuts. For girth as well as furriness. Here was some definite *Trouble with Tribbles.*

GAB was making another round, there was nothing for it, Service would have to touch these freaks of nature, these abominations to humankind. He considered for a moment, is that why the Himalayan version of Sasquatch is referred to as the "abominable" snowman"? Hmmm, made sense, but GAB was watching, so back to the task at hand.

Service decided to go with the grip Player[2] had shown him, the one he'd use to throw a curveball. Two fingers right on the seams with the thump opposing them on the opposite side of the ball or in this case the coconut. It would be difficult to locate the seams under that dense matting, he'd just guess, even under GAB's surveillance he was not going to feel around for them. He also decided

---

[2] Athlete element of WC.

to forgo the wrist snap that makes a curveball tumble as it crosses home plate. A man, any man, even the man searching for crabs on another man's body, a lowly AB has some pride after all. Doesn't he!? Doesn't he really!?

Like after a bad vehicle accident, Service has blacked out most of the testicular expedition from his memory. He only remembers that it was traumatizing in the extreme. He got through it though, thanks to God, the real one and GAB and the power of 50. He remembers the traverse across and down the legs, including those freakishly furry toes, but it is not worth describing. That portion of the ordeal pales by comparison to the horror experienced in the more northern climes.

Having been experiencing empathetic terror from the event as Service relived it for my, and ultimately your edification, I began to relax some, thinking that the worst of it was over now that all of the hair had been cleared. This did not, however, abate my shock and appall. I was without an appetite, which would not reappear for a couple of days, I was to learn. Service told me that he had lost 10 pounds over the next few days following the follicle holocaust due to nervous evacuation of multiple varieties and the inability of his digestive system to process any form of nourishment. In any manner, my

1-30

Crab

sphincter had begun to relax and Service noted my diminishing tension.

"Oh, you think that was the worst of it!?" he queried. "Not so, my friend." It had been a thoroughly gut-wrenching action, but by no means had all the danger passed. The fear of further humiliation held fast. "What was yet to be, while not so graphically horrible, was fraught with even more peril", Service said.

Service still had to endure the receiving end of the inspection. What's the big deal, you wonder, after, well after, you know, after "that"? Service would beg you to consider the list of potential bad results from having your follicles felt up in the presence of 50 brethren.

First and foremost, what if he liked it? What if he got a Boner? What if it tickled and he reflexively giggled or if in an effort to isolate himself from the here and now he went to his "happy place", daydreamed too much and unconsciously grinned or smiled?

Service needed to expend all his remaining emotional strength to maintain a look on his face which suggested he was undergoing an extended proctological exam in a "teaching" clinic where a student was being allowed to take his very first stab at performing the procedure.

1-31

Crab

Unpleasant yes, but necessary not only for Service's continued well-being, but also for all of those who would be grateful for the new doctor's highly skilled, well-trained fingers someday. Yes, Service would have to bear it and maintain the stern expression of one who is doing something good for all of mankind. Service did not have access to Gerydomo's culturally inbred stoicism. Gerydomo is a Native American element of WC who featured in the afore mentioned recurring dream last had by Service. He might have to imagine nuns doing very bad things to maintain his posture of mild indifference. A pity, Service reflects now, that at the time he did not yet have access to the shared memories and abilities of all the elements of WC set.

Even though he was somewhat ticklish and without the silently, smoldering strength embodied by Gerydomo, Service bit his lower lip and suffered his own examination without reaction. More than a mean feat when one considers the fuzzy fingers of Uramaya Yeti. That freakin' Sasquatch! Mostly, Service used the indelible image in his mind of the dark, wrinkly, grayish, sweating cleavage that separated the ancient and enormous breasts of his first-grade teacher, Mrs. Jeters.

Throughout the years this had proved even more effective than images of bad nuns when he needed to

1-32

Crab

stifle a grin, giggle or spontaneous boner. It had pretty much become his go to move for that purpose. I have heard Wryder, namesake character element of WC, concur on several occasions that this imagery is still quite effective for inducing the glazed over appearance of indifference to what was happening in the present. It would occasionally induce vomiting as well.

"Buddy check" complete the ABs were called back to attention, told it would be repeated each morning and each night, just before lights out for the next three days. If at the end of that time a single crab were found on laundry or person the entire flight would be restricted from transferring out of basic training and moving on to the tech school each had recently been assigned to. When leaving as soon as possible had become your only goal in life, this had both the demoralizing and motivating force that had been hoped for.

If there was a crab on Sasquatch, by God and by GAB, he, Service, would find it. His country was calling, and hadn't he signed up to meet that call in the first place. Heroes don't choose their missions, they just adapt, improvise and overcome to complete them.

Okay, a little embellishment on my part, a tad over the top, maybe. All Service told me was that he sure as hell

1-33

Crab

wanted to get out of there and he was pretty pissed off that he might not, because of some little bug, some tainted poon that he hadn't even been in on. If he'd ever thought life was fair, he didn't anymore. They were finally told to go to bed and sleep the remaining two hours before revelry.

It's doubtful anyone slept, the scratching noise was too loud. That same stupid Ohioan got up and went pee again. A couple of hours later the flight was standing at attention at the foot of their beds once more. Each anticipated with an extended range of emotion from abject terror to mild delight[3] the command to "Buddy check!" If only life were so simple. If only the powers that be, in this case GAB, would set the rules and then leave them alone. "Please stop changing them just as one has acclimated himself to the circumstance", Service bemoaned. A new wrinkle was about to be added to the buddy check.

During the flight's two-hour regeneration phase, GAB, or more likely a flunky of his had procured from the dispensary some anti-crab or crab killing, nuclear shampoo of some sort. It was to be dispensed to the flight of un-cleans. But, as they say, nothing in life is free. Not even fucking crab fucking killing fucking shampoo!

---

[3] Therein lies a Chronicle for another time.

Crab

The new rule was this: to obtain some of the magic elixir, whose main ingredient was apparently gold, you had to prove you were a carrier. The only way to do this of course, was with a live specimen. Each AB was issued a 1.5-inch piece of scotch tape. You would check your buddy and when a critter had been flushed out of the bush, this whole event having had taken on a slight Safari like tone to it at this point, you had to somehow adhere it to the piece of tape. A cadre of GAB flunkies were brought in to observe and ensure there was no cheating and not all 50 crabs were pulled from Johnny and distributed amongst the men. The ABs had by this time learned to work together when they had to. Johnny having been the original carrier and having a pelt second only to Service's buddy, ol' Squatch, for density, was a virtual crab motel. The tiny creatures were fairly jumping off him and in just a few seconds his piece of scotch tape was no longer transparent, looking more like a piece of black electrical tape.

As it turns out, spotting and snagging the little bastards is one thing when they are plentiful and active like on Johnny where overcrowding had caused them to begin shoving and pushing each other out into the open. It is quite another to adhere a live one onto a piece of tape after they have been tormented by hot water and chased

1-35

Crab

deep into the bush. What the hell could you bait your tape with? A couple of ABs set their trap by merely sticking the tape to their pubes and waiting for something to walk into it. As noted, the beast seemed to have taken refuge too deep in the bush by now for this technique to be effective. Besides, one paid a substantial pain penalty upon tape removal if the screams Service remembers hearing were any indication.

Most attempts were fruitless, or crabless, so not many of the ABs were not going to get the nectar of salvation, though they all felt the itch for it. That incessant itch. Desperation set in and a black market for crab bearing tape evolved spontaneously. Lifelong friendships were cemented in those few moments. That stupid fucking kid from Ohio, the one with a weak bladder, got caught trying to smuggle one off his buddy in from the latrine on a Band-Aid he'd had the buddy apply. The stupid, gutless bastard hadn't even nicked himself to draw blood and lend a little realism to his scheme. So, the crackdown came and severe penalties were announced for anyone caught trying to run the crab blockade from here on out.

The difficulty in catching them soon became apparent even to GAB as only six or seven ABs had verified specimens. Johnny's personal catch skewed the average to about 20 per AB for the flight and with that many

1-36

Crab

about, there had to be more than six or seven guys carrying some.

In less than a week, if the present situation could be cleaned up, all the ABs were scheduled to go to various tech schools, to become specialists, experts in an assigned field. A mechanic or aircraft electrician, for example. Some of them already were specialist. Some of them already possessed the quick snapping fingers and innate ability to think like a body crab, anticipate his movements and capture him. A God-given talent, one would assume (the real God, not GAB).

In a magnanimous and uncharacteristic gesture, GAB allowed that these few experts would specialize in performing the searches. They would go in and only remain on station until at least one of the enemy was captured or until the area had been completely scanned. Service reverentially thanked God for his slow fingers and un-crab like brain.

Force 10 from Navarone began moving down the rows of beds. Some of the patrols ended quickly with the capitulation of a crab in the first minute or so. A few were exhaustive, requiring a thorough search before populating the tape. Even fewer, only five or six, produced no crabs for further interrogation.

1-37

Crab

Not at all surprising one of the expert trackers, the most prolific capturist in fact, was Johnny. He was hauling them in like a grizzly bear in a salmon run. His appearance being not all that much different either.

 Most of the ABs who were desperate for the itch relieving, medicated shampoo clambered for Johnny to search them, "do me, me next", they pleaded. If one of the other trackers failed to turn up any crab sign, Johnny was called over to renew the searchee's hope. Six times out of seven, damn if he didn't come up with at least one bug.

As force 10 continued to move down the row towards him, Johnny performing his heroics and marking tape with tiny, dark spots as he came, Service considered the odds. Why was this dimwitted, over follicle festooned, yard o' shit eatin' motherfucker from Mississippi so good at catching crabs? Why so much better then all these other, more humanoid ABs?

Experiencing an epiphany and with a bolt of clear reason, Service made one of the few decisions of his life, certainly the first one he'd made since being in basic training. Johnny would not "do him". Service would mill around, step back to ensure the luck of the draw did not land

1-38

Crab

Johnny on him or anywhere near his pubes. When, and he believed it would be when and not if, one of the other examiners pronounced him clear, he would buck the odds, forgo the common wisdom and would not seek a second opinion from the crustacean covered crab master.

That was it, you see. Johnny wasn't finding them on his fellows, the little bastards were running down his hairy fuckin' arms and leaping across to a new host. It was this migration that was filling all the tapes. Everyone else's pubic patch was the West and Johnny's arm was a fucking wagon train. In his mind, Service could see the little devils hitched up and pulling a Conestoga full of their eggs to the new promised lands.

Just as he had originally been, Johnny was still the carrier. Typhoid Mary, Craboid Johnny, it was all the same principle.

By the end of the inspection, Service was one of only five who still stood with clear tape. Foolishly or bravely, only history would be able to declare which. "The others, the Johninites got their doses of shampoo and marched naked to the shower. We few, we proud, we band of brothers stood solemnly waiting our turn to shower", Service told me.

1-39

Crab

The standard buddy checks, not those done by the expert crabsmen, continued morning and night for the next three days by which time all sign of the crab infestation had been eradicated. With little fanfare, the orders were issued at the end of the week, each AB went off to their assigned technical training base and BMTS (basic military training squadron) 3802, flight 163 was no more.

Service never kept in touch for any length of time with the other members of flight 163 and would probably not even recognize them if he were to see them now. But, there is one hairy penis and set of balls he will be able to identify for the rest of his life.

Chapter 2 Dash

A Motorcycle Chronicle from the Wryder Collective Featuring Player (circa 1970).

In this Story Player is the 14-year-old athlete and competitor substrate element of Wryder.

Player couldn't run, couldn't jump and couldn't keep time on the bass drum. Worst case of white man's disease ever imagined. Still, he played all the sports and had even attempted drumming. That had been a disaster, endowing himself and his family with utter shame.[4]

Running and jumping are relative skills it is to be supposed. Player could make the physical motion of doing each, but the motion was slow, laborious, and had little effect in propelling him either horizontally or vertically. His normal teammates and coaches always thought he was loafing or goofing around. It did not seem possible to them any ancestral lineage that could yield as inept of a physical specimen as this should have been able to weather the challenges of evolution and still be around

---

[4] This episode is detailed in another Chronicle called, *Louder.*

to conceive such an individual so ill-equipped of physical prowess.

Player attended a small school however, often fortunate that it could even field a team. They were in a league of schools with similar situations and played a modified form of football that utilized only eight players per side rather than the normal 11. "All the sports", meant football, basketball and baseball. There were tenuous efforts at wrestling and track as well and occasionally they were able to field a team.

The limited talent pool virtually guaranteed that you made any of the teams you tried out for, so Player made the football, basketball and baseball teams. He once even made a hapless foray onto the track team where he was used to fill out the field in races with so few legitimate entries that just showing up and completing the run garnered a half or quarter point for the team. This saved the other "runners" strength for the races they had the best chance of winning or scoring whole number points in.

Player's role as designated race booby prize winner was the most humiliating of all his competitive athletic experiences, but he was able to tolerate it. He told

2-2

Dash

himself the running was getting him in better shape for the sport he particularly loved, basketball.

Yeah, he could handle the shame and embarrassment, the anticipatory dread of knowing he was going to come in dead last every time with nothing he could do about it. His only hope rested with intervention of negative aspect. Someone else in the field would have to blow out a knee or pop an Achilles tendon. Even if that happened, he still only ended up next-to-last. The possibility of the entire rest of the field pulling up lame was quite remote. Although he felt like the coyote of Road Runner Cartoon fame, this was real life, no freaking cartoon.

Yeah, he could handle humiliation. Besides, the coach stuck him in the longer races like the 800, half-mile or mile. The field usually spread out in these events and there were always a few stragglers. He could finish not too long after them, by which time everyone's attention had moved on to the next event anyway. He could run steadily and a reasonable distance if he was rested. he was doing three to seven miles each practice during the week. Unlike everyone else, he just couldn't finish before dark, even during daylight savings time.

Yeah, he could handle the humiliation, he was a team guy, this wasn't his sport anyway. Then there was the meet in

2-3

Dash

Slightly Larger Town, USA. It seemed more of the fields were not full that day than normal, so he had a chance of possibly winning an entire point if he were willing to enter enough events.

The coach put him in the 800, not his best event, but he was confident he could get that one quarter point for finishing last and get off the track before they set up the hurdles for the next race. Remember, he couldn't jump either. He did it, he finished in complete oblivion as everyone had thought the race was over when the stragglers had chugged over the finish line. He came in several seconds, nearly a lap after them. Sweet! Only 3/4ths of a point to go for a new personal best. The run had taken something out of him physically, he foolishly had tried to compete with the stragglers for the first couple of laps. Emotionally he was on fire and he was counting on that to pump up his adrenaline output.

Then player learned the 400-meter event[5] already had more entrants than point winning positions, so that took his next best shot to score off the board. He liked the 400, because you could only fall so far behind in one lap. The coach came up and told him the 1600 had a short field, so he had entered Player in it. This was by no means a strong

---

[5] Called the 440 and measured by yards in those days.

2-4

Dash

event for him, sure he always finished last regardless of the event, but only those who always finish last know there are some things worse than being last. Like running and jumping, humiliation too is a measurement that is quantified on a relative scale.

So, Player set a personal challenge for himself in the 1600 he was about to run. He did not want to get lapped. There were four laps to this event, so he was looking at a pretty tall order, especially with his legs already partially fried from the 800. Hey! A blunt-bladed, obtuse splitting mall can lose its edge the same way a surgeon's scalpel does.

At the end of the first lap for the competitive part of the field, Player was half a lap down. The real racers were literally running twice as fast as he was. The math was simple, not only would he be lapped by the "end" of the race he would still have two laps to go. More probably, because the runners would pick up their pace, maybe even kick to the finish. He wouldn't. Despite appearances – and results – Player had started like he was the designated rabbit, the guy a coach puts in a race who has no chance to win, because of the distance, but he sets the pace quicker for the first couple of laps to push the other runners to shorter times for the early quarters of the race.

2-5

Dash

Player was no rabbit, but he had started harder than he should have in his desire to stay close enough to the field to keep from being lapped. That and the "too quick" 800 had taken a lot out of him. Now he wasn't even sure if he'd be able to finish before they waived him off the track. The officials might even do that before he got lapped, so he would not be an impediment to the legitimate competitors, especially if he were approaching the finish line at the same time, albeit the real racers finishing while he was only marking his halfway point.

Things didn't look good. He had to finish to snatch the half point that was hanging out there free for the taking due to the short field. There were three things he had noticed about this race. Ultimately, they would aid him, but he had not quite perceived an entire plan yet.

First, the three lead runners were equally matched and had remained uncommonly close to one another, had even changed leads a few times. This and the distance they were ahead drew all attention away from Player's tentative hold on fourth place.

Yes tentative, because of the second thing he noticed. It was something he'd never seen before. It was in fact quite unbelievable and Player was not sure how to interpret let alone deal with this unfamiliar phenomenon.

2-6

Dash

He had another runner, well – mover, on his heels. On "his" heels. The guy pulled up beside him on the straight, but Player had established the inside lane and pushed him back on the turns. Player had never been in this situation before, he had never actually raced. Who was this hapless bastard? This poor, humiliated, designated booby runner? So, Player's coach wasn't the only one who would rob a kid of his pride and self-esteem during his formative years of manhood for a half, even a quarter of a fucking point at a high school track meet between schools that couldn't even muster enough players for an eleven-man football team! Interesting, true strategists they.

The third oddity of the day was this track. It circled what would be the football field during that season, but was now where the field events: shot put, high jump, discus, etc. were held. The course was essentially an elongated oval with the two long sides pulled straight and the four curved corners sweeping, but essentially making four 90 degree turns rather than two 180-degree arcs at ends of an oval. However, the truly odd part was on the far side of the second turn from the start/finish line which was in front of the main grand stand. There was a second, smaller set of bleachers, the visitor seating supposedly, built over the track. After coming out of turn two and for about 25 yards down the back straightaway the runners ran under this enclosed structure and were completely out of view from the spectators and race officials. It was dark, but amazingly roomy in there. Several seconds would elapse in there depending upon if you were a normal runner. For Player and on this special occasion, the other hapless bastard pacing him it would be more than several seconds.

The stich in Player's side told him that at this blistering pace, half normal, he would not only be lapped, he wouldn't even finish the run. No half point or even quarter point.

Flash Gordon, or whatever this ground sloth beside him was called was really beginning to labor as well and Player figured them both to be in the same boat. As they entered the tunnel, both Player and Flash dropped their stride to a walk, though that didn't change their pace much. Then they stopped altogether, grabbed their sides, bent over and panted for a few seconds. When they straightened back up almost simultaneously Player said, "You know, I don't even want to leave here." Flash nodded in agreement and gasped out something like an affirmation. Player continued, "You know they're gonna' flag us off. Fuck it, let's just sit out a lap and get disqualified on our third lap instead of the fourth."

2-8

Dash

"Yeah, fuck it. Good idea!" Flash grunted during an exaggerated exhalation.

Player peeked out the entrance of the tunnel and saw the leaders coming. He motioned to Flash, "hey c'mon, no use in advertising what we're doing." Player and Flash slid back into the shadows at the entrance end of the bleacher tunnel. Within seconds the leaders entered the tunnel and passed without noticing them. Then they were gone out the other end like a chili fart.

Flash said, "they probably think we're somewhere behind, just entering the tunnel or we got waived off the track already."

"Or they don't give a shit about where we are anyway, more likely", Player bleated. "C'mon, sit down." They did while Player laid out his strategy for avoiding maximum humiliation. They'd sit here and rest until the next time the leaders came through when they would be on their last lap. Flash and Player would follow them in, get off the track and just wait until an official came over and disqualified them. It was better than getting pulled off the track during the race. Flash agreed with no discussion. "There's one more thing", Player ventured.

"What's that?" asked Flash.

"You know, if we finish together it's just gonna' make this thing look even more obvious that we planned it."

"Do you really care?" asked Flash. "Fuck man! We're both booby runners! Fuckin' coach never shoulda' done this to me. I only trained for the field events anyway."

This stung Player a little bit. Hell, this guy hadn't even been running and he was at least as good as Player.

Then Flash said, "Tell ya' what, after they go through, let them get out the other end about 40 yards. That'll keep you respectively behind them and for all intents and purposes out of sight to anyone who might be watching this debacle. You should finish about 100 yards, maybe 200 yards behind them. I'll come out about ten yards behind you and cruise in. I don't give a shit how it looks, but if you do, what the hell."

It sounded good to Player. They checked the location of the runners and slid back into concealment as the runners zipped by. Player walked to the exit end of the tunnel, waited a few seconds and "sped" out after them in pursuit. Flash followed a few seconds later.

The thing played out just about as the boys had figured it would, except for one thing. No officials came their way.

2-10

Dash

There was no talk of disqualification. When the race results were announced, Player received one half point for 4th place and Flash got a quarter point for fifth. Inexplicably, no one had even noticed them dropping out for a lap. They were too slow to see. The officials must have been watching the leaders only to make sure a foul did not affect the outcome. Everyone assumed no one could have gotten that far behind. Sure, they'd finished 75 yards and more behind, but that was not completely unprecedented, it'd been seen before, rarely, but it had happened. It was one of the few moments in life when one's pitiful prowess produced perfect perception.

Flash declared, "Screw this, talk about grim, now I have to look at the score sheet and see my name next to the individual total column and see 1/4!"

"Now another man might have been angry, and another man might have been hurt..."[6], but Player just plopped his ass in the dirt. He had 3/4s of a point, but his legs were spent. He wasn't sure what events were left anyway, so it didn't look like this was gonna' be his first, probably only, full point day. He acquiesced to the thought quite easily, track wasn't his sport.

---

[6] Thank you Harry Chapin

As he sat there, his legs jellied like the Spam byproduct at the ends of the can, the strategy-wise coach came up to Player and said, "Hey, c'mon, there's a short field in the 100-yard dash." Player looked at him like he was joking. He had to be. He wasn't, "c'mon" said the coach."

Player protested, "you know I can't sprint, I can't even run."

"It'll be alright. We need the quarter point and I know you have three fourths of a point already. All ya' gotta do is finish. You can't get lapped in a 100-yard dash!"

Player was inevitably chided into it and shakily got to his feet. Coach, having already entered him guided Player to the starting blocks. He'd never even used these things before. Coach showed him which foot went where and leaned him over, so his hands touched the ground. He was about to tell Player to get his ass down, but saw the starter raising his gun, so he stepped back. Player was now "fully" trained for what would happen next.

Bang! The sprinters leaped forward and were five yards away when Player got his head up enough to see forward and tenuously pulled one foot and then the other from the blocks. Yeah, he pulled away, though somewhere in the back of his mind he recalled you were supposed to explode off using the blocks to help direct your force

2-12

Dash

forward. That took technique and fast twitch muscle fiber tissue. Player never possessed either. His legs were making a sort of running motion, but more like churning, resembling a fly in molasses. He was suddenly, well in a sense of the word, making up ground. Not on the sprinters, just on the track whose end seemed to have been extending away from him during his first couple of strides. The end didn't look much closer, but at least it was no longer receding. He was already five yards offa' the blocks, so allowed himself a peripheral glance across the other lanes to see where he stood. It did indeed look like he was standing, still that is. The sprinters were twenty-five yards gone. This did not bode well, but there was nothing he could do now but run. At the time it never occurred to him to fake a hammy. There was no tunnel to hide in.

At ten yards, they were at fifty-five and shrinking rapidly. What kind of time he was making Player didn't know, but when he was at the fifty yard point he heard the announcer call his name as the 4th place finisher and looked across and down the track to find himself alone on it. Fuck! Who said you couldn't get lapped in a hundred-yard dash?

The one hundred-yard course is lain out right in front and at the center of the grandstand. He still had half of it

2-13

Dash

laying in front of him, only to him, no one else to share the "spotlight."

He could take the humiliation. Player continued to churn, but the finish line began receding again. He could hear laughter getting louder and coming from all quarters. From his own team, from coach. There was some pointing too, not that any further signaling was required. It was enormously fucking obvious who owned the track now, king of the whole pointers.

2-14

Dash

Chapter 3 Homer

A Motorcycle Chronicle from the Wryder Collective Featuring Player (circa 1972).

In this story Player is the 15-year-old substrate element of Wryder.

In a recent chronicle called *Dash*, Player related the high and low lights of his track and field career, the same event conveniently delineating both occasions. However, he played some ball too. You will recall that Player is the young sportsman of WC. Pedaler, WC's perpetual ten-year-old had played ball too and helped train Player, but this is Player's story.

In *Dash*, Player explained that because he had gone to a small school with a limited athlete talent pool he was assured of making any team he tried out for. This is chiefly how Player was able to participate in as many sports as he did. Also, from *Dash*, it is known that Player suffered from both acute and chronic Whiteman's Disease. His running and jumping motions which each had a freeze frame appearance when he performed them, propelled his body neither forward nor vertically with any but negligible geographical displacement. Given this observation, it is likely one would have by now developed the perception of Player as a physically inept, graceless, stumbling buffoon. There is not enough evidence to argue the contrary, but as it is said, "every dog gets his 15 minutes of fame or everybody has his day or something like that." Truly, Player was never a world class athlete or even hamlet class in the final analysis, but there were moments when he did display flashes of Jordanian and Ruthian prowess.

Player is not sure exactly what term or phrase athletes currently use when describing the experience of heightened capability or awareness. During prior years he had heard it referred to as "being in the zone", by Mr. Jordan and other professionals. That is the phrase he knows, so it is the one he will use.

Player can attest to two things, first is that this phenomenon is real. Secondly, he remembers having been "in the zone" about a half a dozen times in his athletic career. Of his three most vivid memories, the ones he can still see completely in his mind's eye with all the nuance, color, texture and smell intact; two were while playing basketball and one during a baseball game.

Player wants to talk about the time he "zoned in" during a baseball game.

Play ball!

All the cliché descriptions of a beautiful afternoon for Spring baseball being true right down to the smell of fresh mown grass and impossibly alabaster white, gleaming

3-2

Homer

foul lines demarking the boundaries of the contest's arena; it was the second game of the first season of Player's membership on his high school's baseball team. WC's baseball career had been on a two-year hiatus since Pedaler had last played in Little League, so it was in fact only Player's second game ever.

It was a home game. The same usually inebriated fan, real name unknown, but referred to as Mutt, though inebriated as usual to the usual degree was selected from the crowd and designated as umpire as usual. He always did a good job of it. The more inebriated the better job he did.

The term "crowd" may be an over generous misnomer. There was a fluctuating attendance averaging about twenty-five people. It could sink to fifteen or so if a couple of the popular kids left and took their cliques with them. Baseball did not hold their interest very long. The spectator, not to go so far as to call them fans, count might swell to forty-five when the mill let out and a few fathers and brothers stopped by for a while before succumbing to the siren call of The Only Tavern. That was its actual name as well as an accurate description. There were never more than fifty people at any one time. There was no admission fee or restrictions on leaving and reentering, so the crowd floated in and out.

Homer

Baseball season coincided with the start of Spring Afternoon Drinking Season which followed Winter Drinking Season ending in late March. Spring Drinking Season then ran through to Summer Drinking Season, which really got going a couple of weeks before the Fourth of July. As one might predict, this was followed by Fall Drinking Season and on into Winter as the cycle repeated itself. So, people came, watched a while, left, maybe came back with a sixer from "The Only", left again when it was gone, or the game ended, whichever came first.

"Enough about the fans!" I told Player, "Get to the game!"

"All right", he said, "I just didn't want you to think any of the following events were "inspired" by the crowd. It came from within.

Being a home game, Player and his team took the field first. Player was at third base, because the coach knew he could make the throw across to first base on an infield grounder. It was decent strategy, except for the fact that you had to catch the ball before you could throw it.

Player couldn't field a ground ball if it was tied to his glove with a bungee cord. He'd snag one occasionally, but it was pretty much due to the "a dog having his day" thing again.

Second batter of the game Player got his chance, despite all his prayers that the ball not be hit towards him. It was

3-4

Homer

a hard-hit grounder a short way to his left. Short enough away that even with his limited land mollusk quickness, *remember his Whiteman's affliction*, Player was able to get in good fielding and throwing position. He was in front of the ball, eyes on it, bent at the knees, glove on the ground. Well almost, how that sucker squeezed between the ground and the pocket of his glove as it guided itself between his legs Player never knew.

The horror was instantaneous, a failure like this in front of who knows, perhaps as many as 25 spectators. Then Player heard cleats shuffling behind him followed by an exertive exhalation. Out of the corner of his left eye he saw the first baseman stretching to receive a throw from Player's side of the infield. His first thought was, "oh yeah, I already made a jackass out of myself, now rub it in with a fake catch."

Instead, there was a pop in the first baseman's glove and the umpire jerked his thumb into the air, signaling that the runner was out. Player looked around and saw the shortstop directly behind him in line of travel that the ball had taken. The shortstop was just recoiling back out of a throwing position. He had saved Player's ass.

Player's prayers were answered by the third batter who flied out lazily to left field. No sweat for at least another half an inning as he rolled towards the home team bench. He wouldn't have to worry about striking out for another

3-5

Homer

inning or probably two either. He was batting ninth in the order. One did not bat ninth because expectations of performance were high. Still, he'd like to make contact, at least put the ball in play before being thrown out on a not very close call at first.

The hometown nine would send four batters to the plate in the first inning with the leadoff hitter drawing a walk on four straight pitches. The second batter having watched that from the on-deck circle, inexplicably still swung at the first two pitches which were so far out of the strike zone he couldn't have reached them with a vaulting pole. It was amazing that the catcher had even pulled the first of them out of the air, having had to leap to do so. The second one he could not get to and it crashed into the chicken wire stretched across the front of the bleachers behind home plate. The ball bounced back to him from the recoiling poultry netting before the lone runner at first could advance to second though.

Nerves settling, adjusting to a strange mound or just cranking up the concentration, for whatever reason the opposing pitcher now found his groove. It was high, but not above the letters, it clung to the inside corner of the plate like a starving baby gibbon to a sugar tit. The number two batter whiffed at that third well grooved strike. Batters three and four fanned in succession on

Homer

three pitches each, not even finding the ball to foul it off and the leadoff hitter died at first.

Player grabbed his glove and renewed his "dear God don't let it be hit towards me" incantation under his breath. Coach put his hand on Player's shoulder stopping him after his first tentative stride towards third base. Coach spoke softly, "Player, Mike's gonna take over third base. We need you in right field."

"Need me..., that's a nice touch." thought Player. For anything below professional league and sometimes even then, right field is the baseball euphemism for "you really stink, you couldn't catch herpes from a dozen sore encrusted crack whores!" Well, something like that. The worst fielding player on the team went to right field. Fewer struck balls came to right field than anywhere else.

Player was stung a little bit, but he remembered the adage about being careful what you wished for, he'd gotten it. He spent the top of the second and third innings in right field with no balls coming his way and he caught nothing more than a whiff of rapidly rancifing lasagna made with government commodity cheese, noodles and red sauce reported to have been tainted with trace amounts of tomato being thrown out from the school cafeteria.

3-7

Homer

During the bottom of the second and third innings Player's teammates continued to find nothing but ether as they fanned air completely devoid of anything even resembling a baseball. The opposing pitcher had indeed found his groove.

This brought Player to the plate with one out in the bottom of the third. He was glad the pitcher had walked that first guy back in the opening inning. Now Player would make only the second and not the final out of the inning. Even though nobody else was doing any better, Player still always hated to make the last out in an inning.

Their hurler had been throwing nothing but darts, unhittable, but still all of it in the strike zone, so Player resolved to take a cut at the first pitch. With straight gas working so far, it was unlikely the pitcher would make any adjustments for the number nine lasher in a heretofore hapless herd of hitters. He probably wouldn't even worry too much about location, the middle of the plate was as invisible to these guys as the black corners were. Yeah, Player had already decided to swing even before Mr. High Cheese toed the rubber.

Player had already started his cut when he saw the release of the ball from the pitcher's fingers. His hips were rolling through the batter's box and the 32-inch, Reggie Jackson Model, Louisville Slugger at the ends of his extended arms was coming with them. Just as the bat was

3-8

Homer

completing its slightly elevated above the horizontal arc, pointing its barrel towards the third-base foul line and pulling Player's back leg toward first, the ball vanished. It dropped off the table like a good 6 O'clock curveball is supposed to do. Instead of reacting, he'd guessed and guessed wrong. No need for that, he'd seen the release, seen the wrist snap and the ball rollover the crooked ends of the index and middle fingers, but he'd already committed. Too early and to the wrong pitch.

Player had swung so early that he would've missed it anyway, even if it had come right down the string at him. But wait a minute, he'd "seen" the release, he knew how long the guy's fingernails were. He'd seen the two fingers against the red stitches of the ball and the snap of the wrist, he'd known a curveball was coming before it had taken flight, he just hadn't adjusted to it, because he had predetermined his swing. Player had seen the tumbling of the ball as each set of laces chase the pair in front of it and ran from the one behind it. They'd been easy to see; the horsehide sphere itself had looked the size of an overinflated beach ball.

What was going on here? He'd never picked up a release like that in his life. Might've been a one-time fluke, and ocular anomaly because of the sun being just right behind him and his eyes pinpointed perfectly at the same point as the sun's azimuth which just happened to be the

3-9

Homer

pitcher's hand. He couldn't quite feel his Spidey senses tingling, in fact he hadn't been bitten by anything recently, still colors were brighter, objects closer, and grasshoppers were clicking in rhythm to the singing birds. He swore to God that he could smell which of the cheerleaders was in her 28th day. His senses were acutely heightened. He had experienced this sensation, except for the cheerleader part, once or twice before. He was in the zone he speculated, he would know for sure after the next pitch.

The pitcher had seen his hapless flail at the first strike, just like those of the previous eight batters. There was no need to waste the exertion of another curveball on this loser windmill. He might as well save himself, the way it was looking right now he had a shot at a complete game, maybe a shutout and though it was against superstition protocol to think about it, possibly a no-hitter. He certainly wasn't facing any kind of hitter. Not with this number nine ass clown down there in the box.

Player was already counting the stitches and estimating the ball's rate of spin as soon as it peaked out of the pitcher's gloved hand. He didn't need to see it airborne, he could tell by the guy's grip what he was going to throw. He was trying to serve the high cheese, but dropped down and landed too far forward of the rubber on his delivery. Player predicted this thing was coming right

Homer

down the middle and confirmed that thought when he noticed the ink in the letter "a" of the "Rawlings" tattoo on the baseball was a little smudged. This was the juiciest pineapple he'd seen since T-ball.

The head of Player's bat and ball came together like the opposite poles of two magnets. It was an excellent cut, just short of perfect. Player could feel the compression of the ball and then the instant recoil as it made a 180° change of direction. The bat felt so good, charged like morning wood, full power. He hated to drop it, but knew we had to head for a base.

The projectile coming out from home plate had wings and flew over the centerfielder's head who had not been expecting anything deep from the nine hole. The other projectile, the base runner, launched from the batter's box, perhaps not so much with wings though. The reader may recall the description of Player's running prowess. Player rambled towards first and rounded the bag. The fielder had retreated to where the ball was still just barely rolling, but he still had to scoop it up and turn to throw.

Player was nearly 1/3 of the way from first to second already, with what could be called his "momentum" up if one wanted to be charitable in description. He made a quick decision, concluding there was no time like the present. Base hits were rare for him, let alone extra-base hits. Even if he got thrown out it would still be officially

3-11

Homer

recorded as a single; thrown-out, eight — four (centerfielder - second baseman) trying to steal second. He pumped his arms and his legs sort of moved too.

Second base slowly got larger like the sun coming up over the Eastern horizon. The ball thrown from centerfielder doing the same thing, however it's day seemed to be getting started a little more quickly. Player could see its details nearly as well as he had when it was hurtling towards him at home plate. It would be a close play. Shit! He was gonna' have to slide which did not bode well for a runner whose torso was constantly a half pace ahead of his legs. Of course, there was always the classic headfirst slide à la Pete Rose. He'd used that before and on the one hand, it suited his "running" style. On the other hand, headfirst, usually translated into face first for Player; either into the bag or into the dirt.

Player just quit moving his legs and dove. It wasn't a classic slide in the sense that he didn't skid across the ground, simultaneously moving closer toward second base. Once he hit the dirt, rather than a slide it might be best described as a face plant dead stop. FPDS is how it would be recorded in the official scorebook. Though windless at this point due to strenuous and unplanned exhalation initiating from the ground/abdomen contact point, Player extended his arms toward the bag feeling for it with his fingers. Hey, where the hell was it? He

3-12

Homer

pulled his face out of the dirt and cranked his head back to see sanctuary about 3 inches beyond the full extent of his outstretched middle fingers.

Christ on a bike! This was a freaking cartoon and Player was not too fond of the jackass that was drawing him right now. With panic born from the fear of utter humiliation in his heart, Player lifted himself onto his elbows dug his toe cleats in and lunged forward. He felt the palm side of the second knuckles on his right hand settle down on the dusty, canvas sack just before the backside of the ball confining pocket on the second baseman's glove swept across his arm.

Safe! Good call ump. The sweet nectar of life began to roll down Player's chin and that helped wash some of the dirt off his face. Maybe it wasn't nectar. It might have been some of the tobacco juice that had spilled out of his mouth when he hit the ground. This was as vile and disgusting a habit as there could be, so naturally Player and some of the other guys had been compelled to try it. What hadn't spilled out of his mouth had gone down his throat in the form of a blessing very well disguised. Player's experimentation with chewing tobacco had ended by the top of the next inning, which began right after the 2 batters behind him struck out and left him stranded at second.

Following two slow rolling groundouts in the top of the fourth, a can o' corn fly ball skied into right field about 20 feet beyond the edge of the grass. It was so high that even Player was able to saunter under it. He waved off the first baseman who was backing up to take it. The ball's flight path to Player's glove was like that of a homing pigeon returning to its roost.

The next couple of innings went pretty much the same with nobody scoring and only a couple of guys getting to first base on each team. No one got any further than that. Player made a rather impressive catch to end the top half of the fifth inning. When they got into the bench, a couple of guys kidded Player about needing to get on his next time up so he could steal second and get into scoring position for the winning RBI hit one of them was bound to get. It did not faze him in the least, he had just tracked and caught a hard-hit line drive while on the run. He was zoning like his deaf gramma' picking up a curse word.

It was still goose eggs on the scoreboard or would've been if they'd had one when Player got to the plate again in the bottom of the fifth. The coach had told him to take the first pitch (meaning don't swing at it, no matter whether it was in the strike zone or not) to see if this guy on the mound was tiring at all.

"Fuck that!" Screamed Player, silently to himself. This bastard wasn't tiring, he was a fucking pitching machine.

3-14

Homer

Player new he had three cuts, that was it, only three chances to swing the lumber through airspace around home plate and hope its location would during one of those three tries somehow coincide with the position of the ball. He was not going to piss one of those hacks away to "see" if this fucker was tiring.

Besides, he could see that ball today. If this pitcher would have had a rap sheet, Player could've picked it out of a stack of them by matching up the fingerprints on it to the ones he could see on the ball. First pitch was belt high, barely in the black on the outside of the plate, close enough to be called either way, ball or strike. The umpire would probably give it to the pitcher since he had been right around the plate all day. It didn't matter, outside a little bit or not this arrow steady fastball was in the hitting zone. It was right where player could extend his arms out for maximum leverage and his hips were ready to rotate like a disco ball. This all did happen in the 70s. His weight was on his back foot. He knew to the micro-second when the ball would cross home plate.

Player's earlier swing and hit had been nearly perfect. This one was. He could see the point of contact between the ball and the bat. It felt like morning, noon and evening wood all wrapped into one and then released simultaneously. Who wanted sex when you could have this? The palms of his hands still wrapped around the

3-15

Homer

handle of the bat were giggling like puppy paws on grass for the first time. The muscles in his legs, hips and arms were slapping each other on the back saying, "Jolly good boys! Jolly good!" The English affectation concerned Player a little, but they were probably drunk from adrenal excretion. His brain was about to call out, "more adrenaline, more adrenaline for me and my muscles!" when it recalled he had to run the bases.

This was a baseball field, not a park, which is to say there was no outfield fence, no automatic round-tripper, and no home run trot. When the ball got over the outfielders heads it just went as far as momentum would carry it. However long it took a fielder to retrieve it and get it back to home plate was as long as the batter had to make the four-base circuit. While the ball was still in flight, Player realized he had to run, but man that ball was in flight for a long time. Damn that no fence! He'd been practicing his "bottom of the ninth, one run down in game seven of the World Series, two out, one on, full count" home run trot for years. Eat shit Bill Mazeroski!

There was no fence per se, but there were vestiges of such. If a ball was pulled down the left field baseline and hit far enough it would clear an 8-foot wooden fence that separated the baseball field from the rodeo grounds. In a regular park it would be into the corner bleachers, so if you hit it there you could still crawl and it would be a

3-16

Homer

home run, so they just called it a ground rule round tripper. The batter got his trot and play resumed.

Player's pitch had been on the outside of the plate, so his blast was heading for right field. There was a chain-link fence surrounding the bus garage out that way, the gate opening aligning with the first baseline. The fence ran approximately perpendicular towards dead center field. The thing was at least 600 feet from home plate at its closest point however.

Player was churning for first and he could see the ball still in flight, bearing towards the bus garage. Rounding first, having had to break stride to touch the bag, Player glanced to his right. Son of a bitch, the ball had landed over the fence, bounced up and off the bus garage and ricocheted in the direction of the gate. It stopped about 15 feet short of it on the centerfield side. Player swiveled his gaze 180° to the left expecting to see the ump waving him around, signaling it was a home run.

Nothing, he was doing nothing but watching. Really, he wasn't going to call this!? Hell, it was much farther than the rodeo grounds. He found out later that the situation hadn't come up before, so was not included in the ground rules, those rules unique to a field. It had been agreed to beforehand that anything over the rodeo fence was a homer. The bus garage fence had not been considered as a possibility.

3-17

Homer

Technically speaking, Player's ball was still in play and it would have indeed been just a technicality for anyone else but Player. Him stretching it into a home run was not a given. He had just rounded second base by the time the right fielder had run around through the bus garage gate and was picking up the ball. That kid was fast.

The right fielder threw the ball over the fence and as far as he could towards home plate. The center fielder caught it as he had moved over to set up the relay to home. About the time he had turned to set himself to throw, Player was within diving distance of third base, but he had no intention of slowing down or speeding up, unfortunately. He blew, relatively speaking, past third base. If he didn't turn this bombastic blast into a home run, he'd never hear the end of it.

The ball was in the air, halfway from the center fielder to the second baseman who had moved out a few feet onto the grass for the second stage of the relay. At the same time Player was halfway from third to home. Player was trying to decide if he was going to need to slide/dive or not when the second baseman launched the ball on its final leg of the relay to the catcher.

Fuck the slide, Player knew from Pedaler's experience at the catcher position that this guy would be looking out of the corner of his eye to see if the runner was going down

3-18

Homer

or coming on like a snow plow. He probably wouldn't even catch the ball.

Player beat the ball home by step and a half, but it wouldn't have mattered, because he crashed into the catcher like the Titanic into an iceberg. There was no way that kid could have held onto the ball even if it had gotten to the plate before he went ass over tea kettle.

Player returned to the bench, receiving some handshakes, cheerful congratulation's, but some smartass stuff too, complimenting him on his home run trot or telling him how it'd been like watching a guy on a treadmill. It didn't matter, he could take the humiliation. It was just the opposite pole of adulation and it seemed varying degrees of both were always present.

Anticlimactically, Player ripped a long fly ball in his last at-bat, but the outfielders were playing deep this time. The centerfielder turned and ran back on the ball. Then he jumped and snow coned it right at the peak of his leap. It was a fantastic catch, you could see three fourths of the ball sticking out of his glove. Player couldn't feel too bad about making an out like that. Besides, his home run had been worth a full point and it had held up as the game-winning hit.

Chapter 4 Ant

A Motorcycle Chronicle from the Wryder Collective Featuring Learner with Player as a silent witness (circa 1971).

In this story Learner and Player are the 15-year-old substrate elements of Wryder.

As Learner stood in a small stand of timber he was less than three miles on a direct line from the Sickman Ford Bridge. He wondered if there was any significance to this as a new escapade unfolded about him. Probably not he concluded, but a lot of his history had been logged within a short radius of that bridge and he felt an odd connection to it. Just coincidental geography he ultimately decided. This small patch of large fir trees was the final remnant of a forest left in a grant of land that belonged to school district 400. It was about 200 yards behind the high school Learner attended. All the students referred to it as "The Woods". It was a favored location for lunch break, periods when one had no classes or when one had otherwise managed to become invisible for a time. It was of course loathed by the teachers and school staff.

The multitude of sins, merely perceived and otherwise that this miniature glade, only about 150 yards by 150 yards, could conceal was incalculable. Everything from childish versions of "show me yours and I'll show you mine" to adolescent intercourse to drinking and smoking tobacco or other more mellowing combustibles when available, to the settling of disputes, to curious, bizarre, uniquely teenage, spellbinding acts of bravado on a dare or bet.

It is one of these acts that Learner still recalls with such vividness that he continues to be impressed by it nearly 50 years later. It was such a foolish, ridiculous, inane thing to do, having virtually no redeemable social value and was driven by the purest and most obsessive of adolescent male motivations, horniness. He will relate it now.

Learner was a freshman at the time, as was one other of the five friends who were with him for the feat about to be described. Fellow witnesses included a couple of sophomore friends, one junior and of course the featured player who was a senior. The senior was dating a cheerleader at the time, presumably was even in love with her, but of more import really wanted to fuck her. Hell, they all did or anything else with breasts. This pretty much was the only thought these boys had 99% of their awake time and 100% of their asleep time. At this point in his description Learner went off-track and mentioned a recurring wet dream he used to have while in puberty and all the way through basic training. What made it

4-2

Ant

unique was that it was a Western, partially in black-and-white and partially in Technicolor. I instantly recognized Learner's desire to digress off-track and must admit to having had some desire to hear more about the dream, but I restrained myself from that want and directed him back on task. Another chronicle for another time perhaps.

The group of young men in the woods were horny. This virtually perpetual state of mind and body largely dictated the theme of their conversations. These conversations were a communal compilation of wishes, desires, half-truths, semi-plausible distortions, braggadocio and out right flights of fantasy (lies) regarding their sexual capacity, prowess and reported accomplishments.

These esteem building delusions were necessary at that time, because there exists one major stumbling block to engaging in actual coitus with a member of the opposite sex, or same sex Learner supposes. It is the prerequisite of being able to talk to them and communicate the goal or the end game of their verbal intercourse which is of course, nonverbal intercourse. During the time Learner speaks of, this was especially so for himself and for the rest of the group in varying degrees, he suspects. While not evident by this current narrative, Learner has not always been the suave, sophisticated, socially mature devo of the documentary he comes across as now. The only one in the little gang in the mini forest who had any real expectations of pulling off such a lofty goal in the foreseeable future was Senior. He already had the romantic "relationship" established and the experience in theory anyway and he had been banging away at the chastity door for some time with the cheerleader. The hinges of that hatchway were beginning to falter.

It was brought up for conjecture within the group and a consensus arrived at that one more date, a movie, or dinner for example, followed by a trip to any of the many isolated roads in this rural area that served as de facto "Lovers' Lanes" should provide the final impetus for breaching the last impediment guarding the inner sanctum. The Holy Grail of adolescence, so to speak. Aye, but here's the rub.

Cash, Senior had no cash. It is said money can't buy happiness, but Learner's experience leads him to argue that notion. What he saw that day would be one of his earliest lessons confirming the extraordinary lengths people will go to for the attainment of coin. It helped to confirm his belief that at the very least cash rents a lot of happiness and it sure as hell holds a lot of misery at bay. This seemed entirely obvious to him as he saw the tremendous lengths Senior went to obtain some cash and in turn his true desire.

4-4

Ant

Not totally unlike the Merry Men of Sherwood Forest, the young band knew mischief was afoot. They would see something to make the splitting of a bulls-eyed arrow by another landing precisely in the string groove of its knock to look no more spectacular than a heron hitting a pond with its reflexive take off excrement. In their small bit of forest there were numerous and amply apportioned ant hills. One in particular was of cathedral dimensions, you know, for an ant. It was 8 feet along its major horizontal axis, 6 feet on the minor one and varied from 2 to 4 feet deep throughout most of its vertical dimension. The group was awestruck by its girth and was it ever busy. Literally, as busy as an anthill. These were not fire ants or huge, ferocious red killers migrated north from some equatorial jungle, but there were a lot of them and nobody in their colony seemed to be stopping to smell the roses or take in the fresh air. They were scurrying.

How the following thought ever came to Senior's mind or what the amplitude of the raging hormonal forces driving him to vocalize it must have been, Learner has never been able to decipher. Senior stated in a tone of Spartan-like confidence, "I'll bet I could lay in that anthill for 10 min. without moving." The boast had sounded more like a proclamation and was scoffed off as not being serious initially. It was dismissed with a "no one can eat 50 eggs" air of ridiculous finality. Senior did not flinch from his

4-5

Ant

declaration and the boast slowly begin to assume the reality of a serious challenge to the boys. Skeptically at first, the boys nonetheless allowed into their thinking the possibility that he may indeed be serious. With this change in paradigm now including, "someone might at least try to eat 50 eggs"[7], the discussion turned to particulars, "the rules". Borrowing once more from the career of Paul Newman, "there ain't no rules in a knife fight Butch"[8], but there sure as hell needed to be rules in an anthill lay.

The negotiations went smoothly, concluded quickly and thusly:

1) Laying in the anthill meant that no part of any bodily extremity extended beyond the perimeter of the ant hill that was less than 2 inches deep.

2) First caveat - At initial contact with the hill some squirming, not to exceed 30 seconds, would be allowed to contour the hill into a semi-comfortable fit.

3) 10 min. to be timed by a designated spectator and initiated when the layer's body was in full contact with the hill and had become perfectly still.

---

[7] From the movie *Cool Hand Luke*.
[8] From the movie *Butch Cassidy and the Sundance Kid*.

4) Second caveat - Layer must be on his back, so his face could be observed.

5) Movement was constituted as any visible muscular activation other than breathing and that was to be slow and regular. No relief could be gained by deep, wild in - or exhalations.

6) The fine print - No mouth opening and closing, no scratching, no head twitches, no toe or finger curling, not even a blink!

7) Attire was to be "as dressed", although Senior inexplicably requested the right to remove his jacket before laying down to which acquiescence was forthwith.

There may have been a few other small points, but Learner could not remember any more of them in detail.

The group was now ready for the show, one they anticipated would last only 30 seconds, perhaps a minute, but no longer than a minute and a half at the extreme outside limit. They began encouraging Senior to get in there, voicing their estimations of how long he would last, chiding him for having accepted such a ridiculously impossible proposition. In contrast to his former bravado Senior now displayed a hint of apprehension. Truth be told, the proposed endeavor was so preposterous to begin with that the boys probably would have let him out of it even at this late point with a minimum amount of chastising. No one had seriously, deep down, expected him to go through with it. Besides, there was always that "let's see one of you do it"" argument he could come back with.

That slightly visible change to Senior's countenance had not been apprehension or an epiphany of sanity on his part. It had been posturing. Please, that the reader of this narrative will recall what it is that motivates young men, and the currency with which that motivation can be transported into accomplishment. Yes, sex and money.

Senior re-proclaimed, "yeah, don't worry, I'll do it, but I ain't doin' it for free! You wanna' see it, ya' gotta' payout. $20! $20 for 10 min.! No movin', nuttin'!" The look in Senior's eyes left no doubt about his seriousness and the purpose for the money was universally understood. Man, that motherfucker or more accurately, would be cheerleader fucker was horny! There were the predictable exhortations to the effect that this level of compensation was exorbitant, but it wasn't of course when one considered the vileness of the act being proposed and the group knew this, so the protests did not last long. $20 was substantial, but there were five of these want to be spectators, so they only had to ante up four dollars each which they did, handing it over to the selected holder. It slid out of their collective hands easily as each expected this cabbage to be coming back home to its own pot momentarily.

A moment of mental preparation, a last clothing check; it had been allowed that socks could be pulled up, zippers checked and anything that was adjustable, such as a belt or shoelaces could be tightened. Anything not attended to at this point however, stayed that way and no top collar button as that would be unnatural. Nobody wore shirts that way in those days unless a necktie was also going to be imposed on the attire. That was unlikely to happen unless someone was dead.

Senior entered the anthill with a sort of modified Fosbury Flop technique. A style still relatively new then, having been used for the first time in the high jump at the Mexico City Olympics just a couple of years prior. He fell in backwards, bending slightly at the knees, but just pushing off lightly, only enough to ensure his feet would land within the earlier specified parameters of the colony. Not jumping so hard that his head would extend beyond the opposite end of the pile. This was an impressive technique and one could see the logic of it. His initial landing zone was almost dead on the position he would have to maintain for the next 10 min. This minimized the post landing "scooching " about required to achieve the correct docking position which in turn minimized the opening of transitional apparel lines. For example, the pre-launch tucking of the shirt maintained its position through impact. How effective of a seal this would be against the miniature marauders remained to be seen. Learner suspected it would be like trying to catch sardines in a salmon net. An additional advantage to the well calculated flop entry was that the impact well cratered the pile to contours conforming to Senior. So again, no "scooching" and no "burrowing" required. There would be enough ant activity anyway without inducing even more by countermovement from the colony invader. The Eagle had landed.

Within a few seconds he was settled, he was still, he appeared focused and confident, but no one expected that expression to last. They knew that in 30 seconds, a minute tops the relaxed pose would have morphed into a twisted cartography of extremely prejudicial discomfort. Arms would be flailing, feet stomping up and down, clothes flying off, those recently cinched shoelaces would be cursed and a continuous stream of expletives would be reverberating through the otherwise silent glen. In other words, it would be marvelous! The adolescent male is never so satisfied with the world, so content with his place in it then when witnessing the utmost indignities offerable being meted out to a close buddy. Just a last slight twist of the head, a small straightening of one leg, a cough and one more eye twitch; the timer was on. The contest was joined in earnest. One unarmored, partially bare-skinned, immobilized, defenseless - less a will that would have to prove itself to be iron - combatant versus a colony of literally thousands. A human capable of consideration, rationalized decision-making, an interloper with intelligence against an army of individual insects. Tiny divisible defenders bonded into a single entity, a colony, a swarm, a multitude of singularity, a cast of thousands constituting a single warrior driven by one and only one actualizing instinct, Defend! Defend! Defend! Vanquish the intruder by wave after wave of frontal assault. However one wanted to put it, Senior was pretty much in the shit now.

As the first few seconds elapsed, Learner had to acknowledge admiringly the convincing look of stoicism on Senior's face. But what the hey, it was early, only 30 seconds in or so. The ants were beginning to disperse across the uninvited Gulliver, but none had yet penetrated beneath the defensive denim pants in which Senior still placed great confidence. This confidence would prove to be misplaced. Yeah, it was early. Senior would have to string together 20 of these thirty second statuesque intervals. Inconceivable!

The number of visible ants instantly doubled, doubled again and then proliferated with the propensity of

4-11

Ant

amoebic cell division run amok in a hormone fertilized petri dish. The population exploded to the point where Learner could not estimate the exponential power at which it was increasing, awing him as the multitude of the ant tribe approached infinity asymptotically. He stood a few feet from the colony watching. Senior lay in the middle of it experiencing the ants on a much more visceral and intimate level.

The apparel lines Senior had hoped would serve as an abutment were breached, proving to have been as useless a defensive deterrent as had been the French Maginot line in World War II and it folded just as quickly. The ants took nor needed any time for reconnoitering. Theirs was not a precision strike, no smart or stealth technology was to be launched. Theirs was a Genghis Khan style, all-out maraud and destroy tactic at its most barbaric. Yet, Learner reminds one to keep in mind the ants were the defenders. It was their kingdom that had been invaded. If there had existed an "all creatures United Nations", it would have been Senior drawing economic sanctions not the ants. Learner mentions this, because he does not like to lose his perspective on morality. He has always opposed revisionist history.

Ants were scurrying all over Senior's clothes of course, but more and more of them were finding their way to

4-12

Ant

epiderma, the ant equivalent of terra firma, that first bare layer of a victim's skin that was so tender and tasty. They were pouring through the gaping gateway to Senior's armpits which were left outflanked and defenseless by the loose-fitting, short sleeves of his shirt. Learner couldn't really see the ants through the shirt, but in his mind's eye where most of the extraordinary event would be witnessed, he observed the wild frenzy of the ants tracking through the jungle of Senior's armpit hair. Were they slowed or weakened in any way by the ubiquitous teenage BO residing there? Learner didn't know, but he wondered if perhaps the BO was an invigorating intoxicant to the ants. Maybe they became giddy and rampaged even more savagely with their tiny, little ant inhibitions down and their tiny ant brains delusional from the fragrance. Who knows about ants, you know, besides an entomologist? Hundreds, perhaps thousands of ants multiplied by six legs each performing the River Dance on the normally sensitive flesh had to have made Senior feel like his shirt was on fire. If it felt that way, other areas of his anatomy were rapidly beginning to feel like blazing infernos.

Again, the ants could not be seen once they had scaled past the cuff of the pants, cloaked by the blue, but rapidly becoming ant colored denim of Senior's jeans. With the outside of the pant legs near completely obscured by the undulating formation of ants it was not difficult to ascertain what must be going on below the cloth. Senior's bare legs were covered by the migrating six-leggers the way the Great Plains had once been camouflaged by the quadrupedal bison. Contrary to the buffaloes' plight there were no nomadic, native people moving with the ants and controlling their numbers. There was no railroad coming through to annihilate them to preclude them as sustenance for the natives. Again, Learner digresses. The most frightening aspect of the ants in the pants was the direction of their migration. They were moving north on masse and with monomaniacal dedication. Whether Senior urinated during this onslaught remains unknown. Any telltale evidence of dampness had it existed was obscured by ant flesh during the event and dry by the time it was over. Likely having been absorbed by the tiny beasts, as a herd of wild asses falling upon a waterhole after three days lost in the Serengeti would exhaust it. Senior wasn't going to say. No matter, it had not been excluded by the rules as a defense mechanism, as long as nothing moved during the process! The technique's effectiveness is dubious at best anyway. If the armpit BO had been like wine to the ants, it is presumable that piss would've been like crack cocaine.

Analogous to the great herds of caribou who, after having completed their annual trek north to the tundra and all of its seasonal nutrients were ready to nourish; when the ants had made it all the way north on their sojourn from the ankles, they too were hungry. Though the endeavor is inherently futile, Learner will attempt to get the reader at this point to comprehend the sensations that Senior was beginning to register. He suggests the following: any readers that have ever had a case of crabs resembling in intensity the D-Day assault on Normandy, remember that experience and multiply its impact by about 10,000. For those readers never so fortunate, well just accept that it was horrendous, move on and remain under your lucky star. Senior's pubic region was like some kind of Antstock, except without the bands. At least Learner never heard any.

Still, Senior never flinched. He was a motionless monolith bathed in an energy grid equivalent to that of a free electron in a field of U232 atoms. His hair oscillated like a waving field of wheat from the continuously mobile infestation, but his muscles remained locked up tighter than a nun's vagina on Christmas.

The last two hours in which the boys had been watching Senior with simultaneous awe and abhortion had elapsed in a minute and a half. With the pubic patch and all its contiguous flesh, spherical and shaftical alike fully covered, saturated and with every nook, cranny and opening explored and occupied in the name of the

4-15

Ant

colony, a second wave of emigration from this region began. It mirrored the migration from the Eastern part of America when it became uncomfortably crowded with European settlers, the more claustrophobic and ambitious of them began spreading west. The formicidae (ants) also headed West, East and North, pushed by the tireless formicidaic stream of brethren from the South. Learner never saw any tiny ant wagon trains. This was more like an Oklahoma land rush with the participants traveling light and fast. The early ants would stake out the tenderest, most moist, tastiest claims.

They rounded both Horns of Good Hip and ascended both the East and West Escarpments before descending into Death Valley from both directions at the same time. The pungency of this landscape, death to humans, again probably acted as ecstasy or even some form of aphrodisiac to the ants. Their scurried movements became ever more frenzied as they evolved into spelunkers, exploring deeper and deeper into the darkening cavern. The ants' frenzied feet fairly frolicked past each hair follicle leaving a tingling sensation as they formed a living, breathing, jostling crack full of itching powder.

The boys studied Senior anticipating an involuntary cough, tick or twitch at any time due to the audacity of the ant onslaught. They were commuting in and out of

4-16

Ant

Senior's low-cut shoes like it was rush-hour in downtown Tokyo with Godzilla on a seizure induced rampage. They mobbed his flesh; each pore assigned its own aggravating ant while more ants jockeyed for position.

No cough, tick or twitch came, Senior's expression was steady and as locked as Lincoln's on Mount Rushmore. The time was running on, his breathing was normal, his eyes remained open and bright. Well sort of, they appeared inviting, to the ants that is. As Learner considers his memory of the feat, the part about the eyes may indeed be the most amazing aspect. At the three-minute plus mark some of the most adventuresome ants, advance scouts perhaps had begun wading into the damp mucous membrane tissue that covered Senior's eyeballs. This soft, warm, damp environment was like a natural hot spring for them. Learner could see, again in his mind's eye, the tiny, smug ant smiles on their tiny ant faces as the enriched emoluments of Senior's eyes soothed their tiny ant arthritic aches. Learner is still not sure how ants communicate, but word of the eyes and their heavenly healing qualities spread faster than diarrhea in a diaper and ants congregated at the new hotspot. Senior never blinked. There were a couple of involuntary tears, no doubt the eyes' auto reflexive response to invasion and an effort to rid themselves of the ocular contamination. This additional moisture only served as added inducement for the ants to party on. Senior never blinked. Ants crawled over his open eyeballs masticating, desecrating, urinating, hell who knows maybe even masturbating all over his thin mucous veiled cornea, iris and pupils, but that cheerleader fucker never blinked. Learner was more fucking astounded by this show of will than the lack of response evoked in any other area of Senior's anatomy. Itchy penises and ass cracks are not uncommon to young men. Most certainly not to the degree Senior was experiencing, but we've all seen the clutching and digging. Pretty much expected if not completely acceptable adolescent mannerisms. But the eyes, the will to not rub them was amazing.

How did he not blink!? It was over 4 min. in now with Senior still steady as a Madam Toussaint wax creation. Virtually every square inch of flesh, every follicle laden patch, and every port of entry was now under siege or had already been overrun. Ants circled about the oddly spiraling, bent flesh of the inside of the ears as they funneled into each auditory canal. Once in a while one could be seen stumbling heavy footed back out with a sticky yellow/orange substance on his feet which was the obvious impediment to the ant's normal, scamperous gait. Earwax no doubt. However, far, far more ants were entering the ear hole then were leaving it. Were they just sitting around in there, laughing, stuffing themselves on

4-18

Ant

the adhesive goo? Were they wandering deeper and deeper looking for an anterior exit? Or had the invitingly aromatic, honey tinted, translucent ear excrement become the ants' equivalent of the La Brea Tar Pits? Were they mired in ear wax so deeply that only the eventual excavation by a Q-tip would extricate them? Learner of course could not answer any of these questions, but he suspected "yes" to all of them. Well over 5 min., approaching six, Senior had not flinched. Still the boys felt their money was safe. "No one could eat 50 eggs!"

The ants' panicky pedestrianism continued as they fairly flowed over, about, in and on Senior's personage, the stillness of which stood as juxtaposed to their motion as do the opposite poles of a magnet. He the repeller of movement, they the attractors of action. The 7-min. mark came and went with the boys still believing their money was not forfeit and that their absolute assuredness about the absurdity of this adventure would be attested to. Still, Learner could not be completely honest without admitting that they, as well as Senior, were becoming just a slight bit antsy. To be fair, the money was never of serious concern. Shit no! Even at only 7 1/2 min. and if Senior lasted no longer, their meager honorarium had already been worth the price of the show. Competition, which a bet is a form of, can be misleading regarding what constitutes a victory. As Learner described it, what was at

4-19

Ant

stake here was more than the money, it was a sense of inferiority, like discovering Superman really existed, but it wasn't you. It was someone you knew and had been on equal footing with, but never would be again. Instead of being Butch and Sundance, you suddenly found out you were Jim to your friend's Marlin Perkins, Robin to his Batman, you were just one of the Pips. As a young man Learner and the rest all wanted to be legends not just to know one. However, there are few avenues to legendom, they are difficult to recognize and only work for one person one time. Is this jealousy? Perhaps, but I think Learner is correct in saying it is just part of the nature of boys. They become men when they learn to redefine the meaning of "legend" and to understand the cost of the title.

But, these were still boys, so only somewhat grudgingly did their disbelief begin turning to admiration and an expanding hope that Senior could hold out for the now only two remaining minutes. His complete stoicism, his granite countenance camouflaged any and all anguish that bore upon Senior's well-being like a sumo wrestler on a late April ice pond. The boys looked and listened for signs of cracking, but sensed nothing.

The ants' attitude had not undergone any such metamorphosis. They were still angry as hell and determined to run the invading goliath bastard back up the beanstalk. Tiny ant sized bits of flesh continued to be excavated from all over Senior's inflamed skin. The moistness from any of Senior's damp tissue areas had been siphoned off and each warm crevice sheltered a crawling compaction of ants.

Some of the colony ventured into the nasal passageway via the nostrils. Senior's mouth remained closed, so this was their only point of embarkation to that region. The indisputable evidence of some of the ants having completed circumnavigation of the airway was only revealed at the end of the spectacle when senior finally was allowed under rule to re-open his mouth and break the ant tight seal his lips had maintained for the entire 10 min. travail. When his mouth did open, a word was not the first thing out of it. An ant was, or rather a multitude of ants, according to Learner. Senior's tongue was black with ants as if licorice stained, but this stain was alive, it was moving. He looked like a Louisiana 10-year-old spittin' watermelon seeds, except these seeds had legs.

It would not be correct to say the last couple minutes of Senior's ordeal passed in relative calm. He remained motionless, so gave no indication to the boys, but the intensity of distress to his system had to have been magnifying cancerously. The boys could only speculate about this. No new bodily regions came under attack for the simple reason that by the 8-min. mark the ants had

4-21

Ant

already exploited Senior's vulnerability in its entirety. Oh, ants continue to crawl from the hill onto the apparently hapless victim, but so few targets of opportunity remained unattacked that the ants just began to pile up on each other. Ants are annoying, but not heavy. It is doubtful that a three-inch thick pair of ant coveralls is distinguishably more uncomfortable than a one-inch thick pair. Learner hopes there is a point at which the human discomfort meter becomes so pegged out that any further violation is irrelevant. If true, Senior was at that point well before the 10 minutes had elapsed. Reaching maximum distress and how long one can voluntarily stay there when it is with in one's means to leave is another matter. Perhaps this is the stuff from which legends are made. It is what men and boys wager upon. Well, that and simply for the cash if one is horny enough, but Learner has told us that already.

After about the 9 minutes some discussion was initiated regarding the possibility of "calling it". There were a couple lines of thought expressed favoring this action. First off, as mind-boggling as the possibility of pulling off the 10-min. lay had been at the start of it, it now appeared Senior was going to do it. If he could make 9 min., he could make 10. It was a "gimme", a short putt in golf. Gentleman shouldn't make anyone prove the

Ant

inevitable. Secondly, even at 9 min. it had already been worth the price of admission. Why make Senior suffer?

The logic of both bits of reasoning was summarily dismantled by the "make him do the 10" thinking faction of the group. The first reason had rested upon the supposition that they were gentleman. Less the reader forgets, they were adolescents and male at that. There were a couple of thoughts opposing the second reason for stopping at 9 min. Simply put, a bet was a bet. They paid for 10 min., they should get 10 min. This is one of the truly great aspects of immaturity, meanings are so much more often literal. As Learner has noted in other chronicles, part of the maturation process is the melding of our beliefs into a sort of emotional/rational personality hedge fund. We buy happiness when the price is low and hope it will rise while we try to deal away despair at whatever the market will bear. Lastly, friendship, camaraderie, loyalty, all that crap aside, the one on the pile was a senior and the rest of the boys were not. Learner must be allowed an extended digression at this point to clarify the significance of this fact.

Ritual

Under the banner of tradition, there had been no missed opportunity by Senior to make their existence a living hell. Nothing vicious or uniquely aimed at them. It was just that certain rites of passage existed, and it was generally left to seniors to make sure these rituals were honored and passed down. Such sacred rituals as first-year men being drug through the mud by the facemask of their helmets the opening day of football practice each fall or the hanging of one on a locker room coat hook suspended solely by his jockstrap. (*In anticipation of undergoing this peculiar initiation ritual, freshman in the know wisely chose well-worn, tattered and weakened appearing jockstraps out of the basket wheeled in from the laundry room each night. Learner was never "in the know", so blindly chose one of the stouter, less shared and cleaner looking jockstraps. To his good fortune in this instance, he was of sufficient girth that one good bounce regained him his grounded status.*)

The voguish descent from the hook once mounted on it liked a prized piece of taxidermy was to bounce up and down until the waistband of the jockstrap snapped; alighting one on the floor naked, less several inches of shredded elastic about one's ankles. It was considered top-notch form if one could stick the two-point landing, remaining on one's feet despite the wet locker room floor.

If the waistband failed to break, one was forced to exacerbate one's bouncing motion into a more violent, bungying undulation in the hopes of breaking the two leg straps loose. These were fastened to the waistband near the forward area of each hip and again, jointly to the rear of the genital pouch in the short area tucked up behind the ball sack at the root of the penis, where the legs begin to separate and the first measurable indentation of the ass crack is detectable.

Typically, the straps would succumb to catastrophic stress fatigue within one or two plunging descent and recoil cycles. This form of release from the hook precluded any type of Olympic gymnast-style landing, resulting most often in an uninspired ass plant on the wet floor. Additionally, rather than unraveled elastic at the ankles, an intact waistband would have lodged itself into one's armpits. An accompanying eventuality was the considerable likelihood that the partially detached penis pouch would have flopped up and into the wearer's face. It seldom impeded breathing, but that was a sword which cut both ways.

Some of the aforementioned waistbands and straps were quite strong and some of these boys were not very big. Infrequently, but not so much as to make it uncommon, a hapless youth would remain suspended, unable to free himself with his own exertions. This was known as, "collecting hang or "" hook"" time".

Directly proportional to hook time, and escalating in severity with it was a vexing sensation diagnosed as groinal pinch. The feeling was chronic, but decidedly more acute at bottom dead center of each amplitudinal downstroke.

In these happenstances, hang time and groinal pinch would wax and persist until the suspendee was lowered to the floor by one of the coaches. It might be assumed that considerable humiliation would be associated with the need for assistance, but like the additional layers of ants, once saturation had been reached, it no longer mattered.

All this lead to the true rite of passage the hook ritual was intended to induce. One was to keep one's mouth shut, not rat out the perpetrators. There were far worse fates for those who did. A liberal layering of Atomic Balm (a topical muscle pain treatment with heat generating properties parallel to concentrated ghost pepper powder) to one's testicles, for example. Alas, discussion of this, the Johnson's Baby Shampoo/urine substitution and other voodoo hexes are left for another chronicle as Lerner has already been allowed to stray too far from his description of the ant lay.

End of Lay(s)

The debate had become moot anyway, because by the

time they decided no slack would be cut none was required. Amazingly, 10 motionless moments had expired since Senior's immersion into the 10th circle of hell. That's the one even Dante did not want to talk about.

The timer called it and instantaneously Senior launched out of the ant pile as if propelled by a Saturn V moon rocket. He was a blur of motion, the Doppler Effect on full display. His arms flailed as those of a bronc rider in a blender. Senior's shirt literally exploded from his body like juice from a freshly squeezed zit. Resemblant of the water curtain created by a wet dog shaking, ants flew off him in streams and clouds as he gyrated. The boys had to step away to prevent inheriting the airborne ants.

Senior kicked out of his shoes so fast you'd have thought they were electrified. The vacuum left in the wake by the instantaneous extraction of his feet from them pulled his socks along in the vacant space before gravity could fly in to fill the void. It was impossible to believe Senior could've shucked his pants any faster even if the cheerleader had been there naked and posed receptively. Modesty was of no consideration at the moment, as it usually is not at the forefront of concern for farting, belching, booger pulling boys anyway. Senior's underpants evaporated from his pelvis.

"The humanity! My God the humanity!" The radio announcer from the Hindenburg disaster was not actually

4-27

Ant

there, but this would have been a new horror unlike any he had seen before if he had been. Senior no longer appeared to be of the Caucasian persuasion, or human persuasion for that matter. Only small, freckle like specks of white skin peeked intermittently through his heavily insulated ant overcoat. He shook like Elvis on amphetamines; congenerous to a Slinky struck by Tesla's death ray.

While it was not known by Learner if Senior believed in any autochthonous precipitation rituals, Learner nonetheless took a quick glance at the sky, scanning for rain clouds as Senior danced with the panicked fervor of the demonically possessed. In any other circumstance a straitjacket and some burly men with a van would've been called for, such did Senior slap, rub and wipe himself while sustaining his rendition of the Itchy Butt, Ball and Beyond Waltz to no musical accompaniment. Which is not to say it was silent in the idyllic glen. Not only was the forest air resplendent with an olfactory overload of fir needles, but it was also saturated with an endless monosyllabic string of expletives. Learner was raised by a man with a laciferous lexicon of descriptive terms and had inherited the ability to sculpt imagery with them the way a different artist might fashion clay or chisel granite. Even at his young age Learner had amassed an impressive resume of odd jobs with companionry of comprehensive colloquial speech patterns, therefore was familiar with the regional nuances of swearing a bloody streak. Learner knows how to turn the sky blue, but he cannot do justice to the hellish symphony produced by Senior that day. Regressive "K" sounds, suggestions for physiologically impossible actions and short vowels swirled in the air driven by a dust devil of obscenity.

He could only harm his memory of it by an effort to re-create it now. There are singular events or emotions in life that cannot or should not be recorded. They are for a live audience only and should be enjoyed for the moment and thereafter exist only as a memory by the souls who were there. For a non-contextual example, we cannot know what was going through the minds of Custer's men while drawing their last few breaths at the Little Bighorn, nor should we know. It was never recorded; however, we can conjecture about it with reasonable accuracy. Learner suggests we do so regarding Senior's verbal vilification of the ants. Think of every offensive adjective, every vial verb, every nasty noun, every communicable contraction and the most awful adverbs you've ever heard and string them together in no discernable order. Bellow them out while sitting on a red-hot ice pick with a pair of vice grips locked onto each of your nipples as you're being coated with melting wax and fed uncut spoons full of wasabi powder with no chaser. Record this, then find an amplifier with a volume knob that goes to 11 and crank it all the way up for playback. Now you may be getting close to the surreal field of obscenity Learner found himself in.

This was not the only sound reverberating from the tiny Sherwood by any means. The howling obscenities were matched decibel for decibel by the boys' raucous laughter. They say misery loves company. That sentiment has always been taken to mean that misery is more tolerable the more it is shared. Learner concurs, but it is nowhere near as funny or entertaining as when a company shares the misery of someone else without having to take a measure for themselves. The company of boys for example, watching a buddy going through excruciating, yet non-crippling, lethal or permanently impairing agony, felt nothing but mirth themselves.

Learner and the rest of the troupe were rolling on the ground or doubled over laughing as the devil pulled the strings and Senior continued to rumba like a spastic marionette. The guffaws, belly laughs, mirth saturated guttural grunts, giggles, chuckles, snorts, hee-haws, chortles, bemused grins, whoops and shouts rang at a volume setting of 12.

The boys' eyes shone so brightly that they might have set the woods ablaze had their reflective heat not been cooled by the torrent of tears streaming out of them and rolling down the boys' faces. The young men gasped for

4-30

Ant

air as each new fit of laughter expelled air from their bodies faster than their lungs could draw in fresh to replace it. Learner cramped up as his body could no longer maintain effective phosphorylation due to oxygen deprivation. Their laughter was so hard that it expelled from their noses as well as their mouths. Liquid, green/yellow rivulets of snot streamed from their nostrils. Better that than ants, Learner reasoned. Ribs hurt, and boys tumbled as their faces streaked with tears.

The band played on as the Titanic sank, so too did Senior submerge into an itchy hell accompanied by an orchestra of laughter; the result of his own personal antberg. The difference being the boys were not in the same boat with him as the band had been on the doomed ship. As Learner earlier noted, that was a why it was ever so funny.

Some of the group eventually regained enough voluntary muscle control to override most of their wheezing, coughing and crying, though they continued to laugh. At that point there was a suggestion of taking Senior's clothes and moving them 50 feet or so outside the camouflaging perimeter of the woods. However, it was quickly stifled by the majority who considered that enough humiliation had already been doled out to Senior without forcing him to make a buck-naked sprint for his ant infested attire. Besides, just for the laughter and baiting him into this situation, which is how Senior would remember it, there would already be retribution enough.

So, the young men, and boy did they feel like they were men at this moment, gathered Senior's clothes and began to clear them of ants. They handled each article like it was a 5-gallon bucket full of something that had leaked out of Hanford. As for Senior's underpants, they were confirmed toxic waste. The kid that picked them up did so using the tip of a 3-foot stick and he pulled his jacket sleeves down over his hands to avoid direct skin contact with the stick. Learner did not think from the kid's expression that the invading ants were chief amongst his concerns. Remember the age and gender of the normal occupant of those underpants.

They began to swipe and shake the ants from each piece of clothing. Pant legs, pockets and socks were turned inside out and painstakingly decontaminated. During the clearing of Senior's pants, his wallet fell out of the back pocket, displaying the permanent condom shaped indentation in the leather ubiquitous to the wallet of all teenage boys at that time. The shoes were banged together dislodging the little bastards who lingered inside of them gorging themselves on various forms of foot fungus and residual toe jam. The other kid, the one who now stood alone, at least 20 feet away from anyone else in the center of his group-imposed circle of safety, or

4-32

Ant

"quarantines area" if you will, continued to shake his 3-foot stick. Occasionally, the underpants would slip from the end of the stick and have to be retrieved by poking at them with the end of the stick, akin to how one might check the mortality of a motionless rat carcass found on the garage floor.

Senior continued in motion like a gallon can of tinted primer clamped in a Home Depot paint shaker. Whatever molecules he had left, the ones the ants hadn't devoured were certainly becoming homogenized. Someone lent him a comb which he dragged across his head expelling ants and looking like an upside-down peppermill in the process. Then Senior lowered the comb. It went below his nipples, past his navel, under the belt line, beneath his hips, he centered it along the vertical axis of his body.

The partially subsided laughter and howling erupted once more with tears flowing, gasping and the same cacophony of symptoms as experienced before by the boys. Being caught staring at another guy's junk, package, penis or whatever you want to call it is typically not a desirable occurrence. Rare is the occasion when it is socially acceptable for nonmedical personnel. Learner emphasizes, rare indeed. This however, was one such occasion. Not only was it acceptable at this moment, it was emotionally demanded. No matter how ghastly, this was also grotesquely funny in the way that only boys can appreciate.

Senior was combing the ants out of his pubic hair. With each comb stroke they were flying out of there like half fucked foxes fleeing from a forest fire. It was obviously uncomfortable Learner perceived, as the fine-tooth comb did not pull smoothly through the short, curly, kinky, and matted hair. The comb would stick on a twisted patch of follicles or on a particularly heavy nest of ant infestation, then break free suddenly causing the pointy teeth of the comb to insinuate themselves into Senior's already tortured penis or violated nut sack. At this he would wince and the boys rolled. Laughter pealed from the woods making one think there was a full moon at the lunatic asylum. Perhaps there was Learner mused.

Pull, stick and stab; pull, stick and stab; wince and laugh; wince and laugh. All the while the ants were bailing out like rats from a sinking ship or brokers from a Wall Street crash. Finally, it appeared all the ants had been herded out of the Pelvic Prairie. Deploying the "scorched earth" policy of retreat, they left an itch in their wake that Senior later described as being radioactive. It had a half-life of five days and he still itched 2 weeks later.

With the ants expelled, Senior turned the comb's teeth on himself intentionally and began scratching with it. He chuckled with self-pleasure and groaned with pain,

4-34

Ant

sighed ahhhhh... in a relaxed tone and swore vehemently, smiled gloriously and grimaced uncomfortably as he surfed that ever-thinning swell between agony and ecstasy. Learner is confident that the song, *C'mon Baby Make It Hurt So Good*, must have been running through his brain. Of course, it hadn't been written yet, but as you know if you've read any previous Chronicles, or ones not yet written, Learner is not above slipping the confining bonds of the linear time-space continuum from time to time. When Senior had finished sating his itch as best he could for the present, he offered the borrowed comb back to its lender. As could probably be anticipated the kid suggested that Senior just keep it.

The shaking of Senior's clothes, banging of his shoes, hand scrubbing of his body, filtering of his hair, nose blowing, spitting, ear probing, crack spreading with simultaneous leg shake, and general policing of his personage complete, Senior began to dress. The kid with the 3-foot stick and the underpants came to Senior with his offering first. Senior snatched them from the stick, which the kid immediately tossed away as far as he could with an urgency usually reserved for an unexploded grenade from which the pin had been pulled 3 seconds earlier.

Senior half-step-hopped into the underwear, pulled them up and then sat down as his socks were handed to him.

4-35

Ant

He had no sooner pulled up his socks then he shot up off the ground with similar ballistic characteristics to that of an R P G, rocket propelled grenade. Senior peeled the underwear from himself in a single jerking motion faster than a magician could have pulled a table cloth out from under a pile of China without breaking any dishes. He turned them inside out and a couple of small, black, leggy, moving, foreign objects were expelled. Apparently, the 3-foot stick kid failed to make as close of a final inspection of his detoxification effort as he might have. If he had been willing to pierce the 3-foot safety perimeter the stick afforded or, heaven forbid, touched the underwear to give it the thorough examination it warranted, the two remaining intruders would likely not have slipped through.

Thank all that is holy to young men and boys that the stick kid played it safe, forcing laughter to boom again as Senior had shed the shorts in the blur of a nano second. It continued as he shook them the way one shakes his foot when trying to get dog shit off his shoe. As Learner has acknowledged, nothing is as funny as a buddy's misery, except of course when it appears that the misery has passed and then an extra dollop is plopped down on the victim's plate.

Learner had never understood slapstick comedy before, he just never got it. He had not developed an appreciation

4-36

Ant

for Laurel and Hardy or an affinity for The Three Stooges that seemed instinctual in virtually every other human male he had ever met. Now he got it. This shit was funny. It wasn't just the humiliation and misery of a buddy. It was also that great surprise, that bonus bit of befuddlement which inevitably occurred. Just when it looks like the worst is behind the victim, Bam! Another pie in the face, or ant in the pant as the case may be. The utter frustration when the victim's expression says, "This ain't right! This just ain't fair! I don't deserve this!" No, it isn't, no, it isn't, and no one does, so what! One laughs, because it's a classic case of better him than me.

Learner is hesitant to assign a moral to this story. It seems a little audacious, too self-righteous or presumptuous he fears, though he is not at all unfamiliar or necessarily uncomfortable with these qualities. He questioned me as he was winding down this little piece of his personal history, "am I really smart enough to attempt the offering of a moral?"

We both concluded in very short order that he was not. Only a little less pretentiously however, he will pass along one of the lessons which was highly reinforced by the witnessing of Senior's ant lay. If someone else is in the shit, particularly a personal tormentor, be he so intentionally or merely as a propagator of ritual, go ahead

4-37

Ant

and laugh. If you never laugh at someone else's misery, you'll never learn to laugh at your own.

At length, Senior was again fully clad and apparently ant free. He moved gingerly as his clothes chafed at his gnarly, gnawed hide like 60 grit sandpaper underwear on a hemorrhoid. Admiration and comments of how unbelievable the feat had been being showered upon him as he collected his money. Most of the praise legitimate, but some obviously intended to mitigate payback for the inane laughter. The stick kid especially had a look of concern on his face. A pact was agreed upon stipulating that this incident was not to be shared with anyone who had not witnessed it in person. Learner has now broken that pact, but in his own defense it is absurdly unlikely that he has been the first to do so. Besides, it's been 50 years, he doesn't even remember all the names of those who were there, and he knows where none of them are now. In the back of his mind, in a quiet, almost lonely place, he likes to believe the woods are still there and the boys too. Hell, even the ants, they were cool!

"That kind of sounds like the end of this story", I said to Learner. "Little reflection, some introspection, an interpretation of what it all means, the nostalgic hint of longing for the good old days, a harkening back to the sense of adventure and promise that only seems to exist in youth for most of us, yeah, I think you got it".

4-38

Ant

"You're right, I suppose", he murmured, "but do you think anyone wants to know what happened next?"

"Next!" I exclaimed, "What do you mean, what happened next? The jackass lay on the fucking anthill and somehow managed not to move for 10 min.! Impressive, yeah, but don't tell me now he won the Nobel Prize for stoicism or some damn thing!"

"No. No", said Learner, "Not that. I mean why he did it. You remember why he decided to lay in the anthill in the first place, don't you?"

"Yeah, yeah? The money", I answered, "but that ain't no way to end a story. You can't make it about money, man it was only 20 bucks anyway. It's the accomplishment man, the fact that he made this wild, impossible seeming acclamation and then pulled it off. Christ man! That's all that got Joe Namath into the Hall of Fame. Well, that and wearing pantyhose, but you gotta' see my point here."

"I do", he responded. "But, it wasn't the money, it was the cheerleader, the horniness that precipitated the exploit. Are you honestly gonna' tell me that most people don't care whether he fucked her or not!? Really?"

"Well", I acquiesced, "matter of fact, I'd like to know myself".

"Okay", Learner said, "you got a good point too though. You know, about that being a good place for the story to

4-39

Ant

end and all. I'll tell you what we'll do. We'll go ahead and call that the end, just like you said, and we'll call this little bit extra an epilogue. What do you think?"

"Fantastic", I agreed, "I've seen epilogues before, usually not for short stories like this, but I've always kind of wondered what they were for. I guess this is it; to end the story within the story".

He grunted, "All right then" and was quiet after that. Learner remained quiet for several minutes. I generally do not like to rush him as there are times when he does not do well under pressure. At length however, the silence became uncomfortable, so I stammered, "well" in an inquisitive tone.

"Well what?" He replied, with a somewhat vacant look upon his face.

"Well what!?" Was my exasperated response. "Well, what happened with the cheerleader?"

"That well, okay, I forgot, we're doing the epilogue thing, aren't we", he declared and in Paul Harvey fashion continued with the rest of the story.

Epilogue According to Learner

To Learner's utter amazement, the sanctity of the anthill pact held, the lay and what motivated it did not become common knowledge. However, the question of whether the boys' money had helped to complete a noble quest or had merely paid for a 10-min. show, albeit a good one, well screamed for an answer. Inquiries were made. Less than full ambassadorial protocol was employed however, with the gist of the queries basically sounding something like, "did you get in there?" Which is not to say all the questions were even this diplomatically stated. Some were a bit more, well, shall we say, "Crude"?

Senior made some small show of chivalry, remaining silent for a week or two regarding his status with the cheerleader. By and by, he inevitably succumbed to the interrogatory pressure and spilled his guts as had been anticipated by the boys. The money had been well spent and well purposed. With at least as much gusto as had been generated lionizing Senior at the conclusion of his anthill lay, he was again showered with admiration.

As Paul Harvey now concludes, "and that's the rest of the story". But for Learner it really isn't, his unwillingness to ever end anything is maddening, frustrating and drives me nuts.

I was about to say, "good job Learner, and nice epilogue" and call it a day when he says to me, "you know, there is just one more thing". Like a fly to July cow manure, I knew it would be hot, sticky and distasteful, but I went for it anyway.

4-41

Ant

"Oh", I said in the most nonchalant tone I could muster, "what's that?"

It turned out that a couple of months after the whole anthill thing and of course the completion of Senior's quest that the cheerleader was now pregnant. This was a disheartening bit of news for the boys, not to mention for Senior. They had all thought he had been smarter than that, but each knew in the back of his own mind that at the ultimate moment thinking can pretty much go out the window. If there is one organ that is not involved with the sex process, it is the brain. Specifically, the brain of an adolescent male.

It was a lesson that Learner took to heart. The obvious implication was that Senior had lost his head in the throes of passion, but Learner as always, is never satisfied with the first and most easily arrived at explanation of causality. This guy had lain in an anthill and controlled his mind for 10 min. Would one vagina do what 100,000 ants had been unable to do? Probably he concluded, but also divined that there was another possible reason.

A sperm is pretty darn small. It wouldn't take much of a hole in a condom for a sperm to be able to squirm through. Certainly, a sperm could squirm through a hole in a condom no larger than that of an ant bite. Learner concluded the following lessons: try to keep one's head in the ultimate moment of passion and never trust a condom that's been in your wallet for months and been exposed to ants.

Ant

Chapter 5 Crush

A Motorcycle Chronicle from the Wryder Collective Featuring Pedaler (circa 1969) with Lover and Worker on the periphery.

In this story Pedaler is the 12-13-year-old substrate element of Wryder. Pedaler is on the later edge of his dominance in WC, but it is his story, because there was actual pedaling involved and this is a transitional tale.

Since its inception the crush has dwelt within WC, albeit with various degrees of consciousness and increasingly lengthy periods of dormancy throughout its existence.

It will continue there until WC achieves equilibrium with the universe or Wryder becomes self-actualized, he presumes. However, there are fewer and fewer triggers, such as the photo recently discovered online by Wryder to wring it from dormancy, so it is time to tell the tale before it can no longer be recalled. Pedaler most tangibly lived it, but also had the least notion of how to deal with the crush. Wryder suspects that is almost always the case, the participant having the worst view of an event, so he may need to lend some interpretation.

Pedaler was 12, maybe just turned 13 when he first started pedaling his bike about 6 miles one way every summer day to pick blueberries. He can't remember how much he got paid per pound, too little he's positive. He

Crush

did this for two summer vacations and picked over a ton of berries each year. It was a hot, humid hell. To an objective observer not really that bad, certainly nothing compared to the burdens of previous generations and it would be remembered fondly 50 years later. But, to a kid one inevitable fact always looms as brightly as a nova star. Your own chores and jobs are always so much more difficult, performed under circumstances so miserable and under such heinous scrutiny that the overall trauma of it is not even conceivable to other kids or adults who dance merrily along in mundane accompaniment to the rewarding missions of honor they are "chosen" for.

This is an axiom of youth, well probably of all ages, Wryder would argue. One is always "chosen". Meritocracy is dead, if it had ever lived. The individual is under fardels such that no man and certainly no child should be expected to return from their borne unchanged. Oh! the things one could accomplish, the wrongs righted, the compensations proportioned and the injustices adjudicated if one were but made Czar of all that are! Waxing off topic is a weakness that runs rampant in all elements of WC.

But alas, Pedaler the poor little bastard was fated to be plopped unceremoniously down in those stinking berry fields, mistaken by the celestial powers as just another ill

5-2

Crush

born waif and nickel grubbing urchin. Life is never fair. So, be one ever so young and naïve, one must find one's fortunes and take one's simple pleasures amongst contiguous objects of similar misfortune. Pedaler found himself with other orphans of common economic malignancy. Also, in company with the spawn of those who thought it wise that their affluent bound progeny should be taught the meaning of a buck prior to insertion of the silver spoon. Origins mattered not; they had all been set adrift in the same supply-less, navigation-less, propulsion-less life boat on the hellish, paroxysmal seas of summer vacation which in previous years had been so antitempestuous.

Peddler didn't care for picking berries much, but he wasn't alone out there like he was most of the other time. Those berry bushes were close together, consequently also were other misfortunates who had been doomed to share with him a three-month swim in The River Styx.

Pedaler was just a budding smartass, punk kid at the time, but Wryder looks back with the realization that it was Pedaler's humble interaction in the berry fields that lay as the genesis of the art of bull-shitting that Wryder now stands as master of. The vocabulary, nuance, timing, alliteration, coining and compounding of words and

5-3

Crush

phrases; indeed, the entire science of phraseology Pedaler helped to invent. The innocuous innuendo, graphic description, timely insertion of the regressive "K" sounding words, the pseudo-sexual insinuation to be sure were not at Pedaler's ready grasp, but they were within his field of conception. Their mastery lay the future for the efforts of Worker, Wryder, Player and the other worldlier experienced elements of WC, but Pedaler had his moments which imbued him with a modicum of impish charm.

It was with a pubescent preponderance of adolescent witticisms that Pedaler first learned to attract attention to himself, including that of girls. As singly as Pedaler mostly lived, as cripplingly shy as he was, and as threatened as he felt by the chance of becoming a spectacle of humiliation for some real or perceived fault or frailty, nevertheless, in the berry fields for the first time he overcame those fears. Albeit it ever so humbly and haltingly. He liked attention, even, or perhaps especially that of girls. It was worth the risk. There would be times when other elements of WC: Learner, Player and even Wryder would flinch from Pedaler's assessment of the risk and temporarily pull back from the romance arena. But, these abatements of effort were temporary; hashed hearts heal, sick psyches survive and pursuit persist

Crush

perpetually. Anyway, it was Pedaler's time and WC's first comely quatrains budded with him between branches of blueberry bushes.

Part two

Georgina is a girl's name as is the shortened version Georgia or even Georgie. When abbreviated all the way down to George, well not so much so. But the George, as Georgina was called, whom Pedaler met while picking the bush next to hers was most definitely a girl. The most beautiful girl he had ever seen or could ever imagine. As point of validation consider that this remains an unchallenged postulate within WC to this day, never having been questioned by any other of WC's elements. Wryder recently saw a picture of her taken as she appears now, nearly 50 years later and she remains that same girl.

George was of average height, maybe a little less for a girl her age. She was a Native American of the Northwest coastal region and had the beautiful brown, somewhere between amber and golden skin that all elements of WC have a penchant for. That elegant, effluent skin was tautened over a perfectly formed and symmetrically proportioned physique both fabulous and flawless.

George's pliable, effete, puerile bosom distended with desirable amplitude and sufficing volume. Her facial

Crush

features exhibited bell curve symmetry devoid of the slightest deviation or defect. With long, straight, waist to upper buttock length, jet black hair and dark eyes that glowed like a spotlight light through Arizonan obsidian; there was nothing about her that did not attract Pedaler.

George's mellifluous and euphonious voice, concordant with the harmonic tunes of a symphony soothed the soul while simultaneously beseeching the loins for a proletarian response. It was as if several voices were cloistered as one evoking polymodal responses from a single utterance. When Pedaler heard her speak he re-experienced every kind or alluring syllable any female had ever uttered to him.

Thus, was the hook of love baited, scented and set into the kind of rhythmic motion that causes the light to dance "come hitherly" before the eyes of the nonplussed prey. The smile; William S. might say, "Ah, there's the rub...", but Pedaler paraphrases, "Ah, there's the smile... the smile that barbs the hook of love, makes calamity of such long singleness, harkens one to the country of Undiscovered Emotion from whose borne no Pedaler returns...". The smile was more than lips and teeth and the occasional tip of tongue; it was one to remain forever young. George's smile was hauntingly shy and frighteningly uninhibited. It scared Pedaler and pulled on

5-6

Crush

him at the same time as a Krispy Kreme donut working on a dieter. Once taken, the barb, the smile, does not allow the spitting of the hook. The game of love was now afoot.

Pedaler no doubt waxes bombastically, but his palaverousness is innate to all elements of WC and he is no lesser an element of it by virtue of being only 12. His language may be retroactively loquacious, but he still speaks from the heart of a mere dozen years.

There was nothing about George that did not make Pedaler want to be with her. She in fact had a crush on him, something he knew and would hear her admit a few years later. She pursued him with an unlikely presence in moments when chance did not dictate a meeting. Her berry bucket seemed always to be full and ready for weighing at the same time as his. Their thirst and need for relief somehow had synched. Eating lunch in near proximity to her was inevitable.

These encounters were not unwanted by Pedaler and he himself was not above sitting on a full berry bucket or starting for the weigh-in wagon only to look down, re-examine his vessel, then turn back to the bushes to top it off when George did not follow his lead. He knew that he wanted to be wherever she was. But guilelessly, that is all he knew.

5-7

Crush

The poor, dumb, pedaling little dipshit. He had no clue what you did with girls for fun, especially this one who seemed to be made specifically for fun. Pedaler at the time, well for all time presumably, had a vague notion of affectionate teasing. In fact, that is what probably first caught her attention, but that was about his only move. His other assets included the aforementioned modicum of impish charm and he was not totally un-cherub like in appearance. A slight natural twinkle in his eyes seemed to promise more than what existed.

Beyond the initial ability to attract attention, Pedaler was as ill-equipped for survival in the romance environment as would be an Eskimo and Australian Aboriginal if they were suddenly translocated. He could barely talk to her, not yet having learned that having nothing to say should not be an impediment to conversation. He was as tentative about touching her as a grasshopper was about landing on a hot skillet. The physical encounters did not last long, were generally initiated by George and left his skin feeling seared, though in a good way like a golden roasted marshmallow. That is exactly what he was, a marshmallow. George was the flame and human instinct fueled by the existence of two different sexes within the same species was the stick from which he dangled.

5-8

Crush

As happened a few times, whenever Pedaler did hold George's hand it was the greatest thing he had ever experienced and he would never feel it again. That is the role of Pedaler in WC, to do it, to see it, to feel it for the first time, but then never to sense it again. Many years later Wryder would feel it again when WC found the love of its life, but Pedaler had to watch. It is okay, he knows the feeling or something very close to it. The first love of WC will always be the only true love of Pedaler.

The balancing of emotion within WC, amongst the various elements: Pedaler, Wryder, Learner, Service, etc. has no unique solution or mathematical equivalency. It is the most non-dichotomous of all equations. Each element of WC knows everything about each other element, but at the same time knows nothing about them. They live simultaneously yet morph into newer elements in chronological fashion. It is never known from which, if any field of reality the time variable should be considered. Perhaps that is why the Wryder namesake entity must exist as a collective.

None of that crap means much to Pedaler, however. His existence is an eternal oscillation between wanting to be with George and being afraid that he'll end up with her. This eternity lasted about 10 days, maybe a couple of

5-9

Crush

weeks. George was never without competitors for her attention and she had no reason to wait on Pedaler and his shy, faltering, insecure, scared shitless, naïve advances.

Before his heart burst however and he got his first lesson in longing to regain that which he never had; there was a moment. It was the briefest and most innocent of experiences, therefore seems an entirely improbable event upon which to base a lifetime of warm feelings and genuine wishes of happiness for an unattained lover. It spawns one of life's universal, solution-less questions, "who knows what will be important to a 12-year-old boy?"

Annually in the small town near to where George and Pedaler lived there was a modest Fourth of July celebration. One of the attractions of this event was the arrival in town of the world's smallest, most drab, ramshackle and most disappointing carnivals. There was a booth where one could pitch dimes and hope to win a chipped ashtray, a cart where Dacron candy could be purchased (cotton was too expensive for this outfit) and a merry-go-round missing the merry and round parts. Then there was the main attraction, the big ride, the moneymaker. This was the machine that retrieved any of

Crush

the Dacron candy that might have been foolishly swallowed.

Enter the Hammer. By current multi-G inducing, permanently disorienting, stomach emptying, brain damage causing rides it would likely be considered benign. Nonetheless, it evoked erratic, momentum breaking motion along both axis of the vertical Cartesian plane and elicited "self-controlled" rotation through the third dimension of the Z axis. "Self-controlled" meaning that if you didn't grip and hold a tiny, zero leverage control wheel with Samsonian strength, it spun like an out of balance Maytag with a pair of Levis stuck under the agitator, continuously but not smoothly. As the direction of the Hammer swing changed from back to fourth so did the rotational speed and direction of the Sputnik sized capsule. The "capsule" or head of the hammer held two persons, but they couldn't be too large and had best be on intimate terms.

In the spirit of a blind squirrel eventually finding an acorn, the same inexplicable good fortune smiled on Pedaler one day when said carnival was in town and said romance was in mid-blossom, about day five or six as best Pedaler can recall. Without premeditation, at least on Pedaler's part, he was standing near the hammer, heard a sprightly

Crush

greeting and looked to his left to be met by George's effervescent smile. His immediate and spontaneous joy evoked an affectionate return greeting and genuinely unguarded smile, but his shyness quickly afflicted him with social paralysis which he attempted to disguise as stoic disinterest. Poor, stupid, little bastard. However, his emotional inertia was more than counterbalanced by George's lack of the same. She was slightly older and more confident, besides being infinitely more beautiful than he. Not just beautiful as described earlier, beautiful to the soul. Pretty and sweet with her emotion borne on her sleeve.

With no conscious participation on his part Pedaler found himself jammed into the Sputnik with George. He does not remember what was said or what was touched, but there was some of each and it was fantastic. It was his first moment of romantic intimacy and that is all he needs to remember about it. Despite losing all the change from his pocket while he and George were squeezed together and hanging inverted like a pair of possums this was the best two or three moments of Pedaler's life.

It would be left to Wryder to eventually find the collective's love of its life, but this was Pedaler's contribution to the quest and helped to define what WC should look for.

5-12

Crush

Chapter 6 Coldcut

A Motorcycle Chronicle from the Wryder Collective Featuring Pedaler (circa 1967) and with Wryder (circa 1997)

In this story Pedaler is the perpetual 10-year-old (or there about) substrate of Wryder.

Prologue:

Wryder obviously, is the namesake element of the collective. Pedaler is one of the earliest known character elements common to the set known as WC and is its perpetual ten-year-old. Because of this, it is easy to observe some of Pedaler's mannerisms, distractions, the strange things he says and conclude, "Aw, look at that, just like Wryder, except smaller. He's copying the adults."

Let us not reanimate the chicken or the egg debate. Pedaler joined the collective before most of the other characters including Wryder, so he is immutably part of them. A few exceptions: Conception, Crawler and Stumbler were already known in WC when Pedaler was discovered, but they have always been quite shy and therefore, reticent to tell any of their stories. In fact, the existence of Conception would not even have been known about had not an account of him been given to Wryder by Conception's closest cohort, Spermy. It is most likely that the later elements adapted their quirks and mannerisms from Pedaler rather than the other way 'round.

All the elements of WC love to dabble with words, to coin phrases. For example, Wryder believes it was Learner who once, when having tired of the cliché phrase, "One man's trash is another man's treasure", coined a new one. It has similar meaning, but Wryder believes it conjures a different set of imagery to mind, "One man's barfin', is another man's scarfin'!" This phrase has not caught on as part of the American lexicon as he had hoped it might. Still, one perseveres. This predilection for new, more descriptive slang by WC's elements can be traced back to Pedaler.

The Tale:

One day when he was about 10, as he always is, Pedaler was in his backyard scrambling up the cherry tree to the precariously anchored fortification he had built there. As he momentarily hung upside down with the backs of his knees wrapped around a sturdy branch, gravity made itself known. It allowed the last remaining small, empty quadrant of his stomach to slip back up his throat, through his mouth and into his tiny brain. This less than 100% functioning organ interpreted the vacant bubble as hunger.

"Could it be? Must be", the small brain first considered and then surmised, "I'm hungry." It seemed a reasonable conclusion, it had been nearly an hour and a half since he had eaten anything. The expression "hungry enough to eat the ass out of a skunk" was in vogue then, but highly overused. This prompted Pedaler to coin his own expression to escape use of this tired cliché. Pedaler was "hungry enough to munch the muff out of a menstruating monkey!" That's quite hungry.

Pedaler righted himself on the branch and slid down the cherry tree trunk to the ground, landing with his feet already moving towards the house. That is one of the benefits of being 10, needs are perceived, plans set and action taken. Very little time is wasted on forethought or introspection. Through the back-porch screen door and into the kitchen Pedaler scurried.

He eyed the cookie jar for an instant, but that dream had been dead for a long time. Nothing in it, but spider webs and ghosts of oatmeal cookies like his mother used to bake. Pedaler had always heard those stories from his much older siblings about how mom used to bake all the time: cookies, pie, cakes... She even made her own noodles and bread. It was a legend, like King Arthur, Robin Hood or the Rock Candy Mountain to him. She was a great mom, but she didn't bake anymore.

Pedaler looked through the cupboards. What was all that crap? Must be what he had heard referred to as staples. Most of it was not food per se, these were the building blocks of food, not actual food. Rice, pickles, sugar, salt, cans of vegetables, other junk and a sack of flour. Man, that flour looked old! He peered into the bag and wondered if the contents should be moving around inside like that.

There was also a jar of peanut butter, but he was not a purist and spreading some on bread, then finding a swallowing agent such as jam or mayonnaise to go with it and then having to spread that around, all that could easily take two or three minutes. He didn't have that kind of time. Man! It'd be like trying to wolf down a bowl of soup and being forced to use a spoon; it just took too long.

Okay, one last chance over there. Hit the antique Frigidaire. This was always a bit dicey. It generally

Coldcut

contained mostly leftovers or unprepared stuff for a future meal. Either way, the items were earmarked for a predetermined purpose or a particular person's (dad's) lunch. Extracting anything from either of these veins was simply not worth the inevitable retribution. One might liberate a slice of something from its backside or take a fingertip of something, but mom was extra vigilant now that she had all that extra no baking time.

Pedaler was desperate now, he'd even settle for a piece of fruit if he had to. No bananas if there were any though, they were too easy to keep account of. Man, this fridge was bare, two or three pickles floating around in a Nalley's jar, half dozen eggs, not much..., but wait, yeah, there was something. It was a thick pack and already open, about half of them gone, so a couple more missing probably wouldn't be noticed. It was worth the risk Pedaler's stomach convinced him. At 10, it was always stomach over brain in any case of moral turpitude or uncertainty. In a few years it would be penis over brain, but the point being that for most males, certainly those belonging to WC, brain would always succumb to the veto of a more powerful organ.

Pedaler snagged his prize, closed the door on the Frigidaire as he was turning to go back outside, already

Coldcut

stuffing his mouth, one bite, one swallow and one step towards the door were as far as he got before his mother's glare pinioned him in place.

Meanwhile in the Future:

Wryder and Brolaw (one of his brothers-in-law) were driving around one day. They were metal detecting, or scouting out a place to fish or some such foolery which eventually brought them to the small community of Mineral at Mineral Lake. There was a tiny park over near the lake and a little store just across street from it. What had caught Wryder's eye however, was the royal blue porta potty next to a parking spot for the park.

With a "pull over or I won't be responsible for what happens, and this is your truck", kind of urgency in his voice Wryder commanded/pleaded for Brolaw to stop next to the blue relief outpost. "Might as well stretch a while", Wryder suggested as he launched himself out of the pickup. "I gotta shit and it may take a while, I been holding it a spell and I'll have to get them muscles to relax now. I hope there's paper in there."

It did take a while. Brolaw stretched and then ambled across the street to the little store where he purchased a bottle of Gatorade and a couple of other items. By the time Wryder had taken care of business and pushed open the squeaky-hinged, too strong of a spring-hung, molded plastic, blue door, Brolaw was standing there with one of the items he had purchased from the store in his hand and offering it to Wryder as a gift. "Here, do you need these?"

Back to the Tale:

In the meantime, or 30 some years earlier depending upon how you view time, Pedaler was staring into an expression on his mother's face he did not recognize. He wasn't sure what it was, but it wasn't Happy or any of the seven other dwarves for that matter. This is when he learned about the eighth, non-publicity seeking dwarf known only to a few and going by the name Pissed. His middle name is Off, so some people just call him P.O. Dwarf. I think he got the name after Snow White snubbed him. Of course, he referred to her as S'no Way Bitch! But I digress.

Mil, as Pedaler had always called his mother, launched a verbal assault he had not expected. What he had expected was a mild admonishment for eating between meals again. What he got was anger, guilt and frustration. How had she had time enough to pre-determine the fate of each slice of bologna? She waved her arms and screamed, "What the hell are you doing!? You can't just eat bologna like that! If you're hungry, I'll make you a sandwich, so you can fill up on bread. I gotta' make that bologna last all week! Don't you ever think of anybody else!? The tirade lasted a surprisingly long time as Mil was not usually given much to anger or frustration in front of her children. Pedaler does not remember it all, but there was one poignant line that stuck in his head like shit on royal blue, porta potty, molded plastic. It still makes him and Wryder chuckle when they think of it.

Mil pointed at him and shrieked, "For Christ sake, you can't eat just the bologna, you might as well eat gold!" It's true, Wryder swears she compared it to gold. I don't know, is bologna sold by the troy ounce? Eventually, Pedaler was sent outside and told to eat his bologna, or gold as he now thought of it. He had offered to put it back, but he had already taken a bite out of both pieces at the same time. Rather than ameliorate the situation, his offer just seemed to piss Mil off even more. At her command, Pedaler did slink outside and he did eat the bologna, to waste it now would be an even greater sin than the one he had already committed.

The flavor was tainted now; he hadn't intended to make Mil angry or hurt her feelings. Knowing you had done that was much worse than any scolding or other punishment that could be meted out in your direction. Pedaler loved

6-8

Coldcut

her and knew it was reciprocated, he'd have to think about her reaction for some time. He did.

Two things clarified in his mind. He had suspected they were poorer then the kids' families he knew. He was sure now. He wasn't wanting for anything, but he stuck that label on himself with indelible ink just the same and Wryder still wears it like a sacred tattoo. It's like a battle scar on an inconspicuous part of the body. Wryder hides it most the time, but displays it as a badge of honor sometimes as well. Pedaler always tried to hide it.

Then there was the other thing that became clear. Mil knew it, felt it too, the feeling he had. She hadn't wanted him to learn it. Who would earmark slices of bologna for a whole week? She would, because she knew that if she didn't then Thursday, Friday and next week would be nothing but peanut butter.

Pedaler thereafter noted many things that Mill earmarked and the fact that his and his father's, but especially his name got stamped on them first. Hers was always last. There are many examples, but Pedaler always remembered the bologna.

The whole business of it, the feeling poor, was silly, because Pedaler was never deprived of anything, but he knew the extent Mil went to, just to keep it that way.

6-9

Coldcut

One of the few goals Pedaler ever consciously made for himself was to not be poor as an adult. Ironically, he never was, but could never wash off that ink either. He had to figure out what "not poor" meant. One day he did and many years later Wryder related Pedaler's earlier conclusions along with the rest of this story to Brolaw.

Back to the future:

Brolaw apparently never had forgotten it when Wryder had told him how Pedaler had defined "not poor". The goal Pedaler had set for himself, for Wryder, the sign that would signal to the world that he was not poor or second-class or associated with any of the other encumbrances of being poor was that when he grew up he would never have to count his bologna slices. He would not have to stretch their filling capacity by always making them lay between two slices of bread, he'd be financially okay to the point where he could sit down to dinner, open some bologna or even pimento loaf if he so chose and eat it and nothing else for dinner. If he wanted a second package, it would be waiting in a shiny new, bursting at the hinges full, Frigidaire. As related to Brolaw, Pedaler had vowed that he would be so bologna rich that he could wrap his arm clear to the elbow and use the sweet, soft meat to wipe his ass if the notion ever came over him.

6-10

Coldcut

Wryder exited the porta potty as Brolaw was extending a gift from the little store and saying to him, "hey, here, you need these?"

Wryder smiled and replied, "No, you keep your smartass, fucking cold cuts!

Chapter 7 Survival

A Motorcycle Chronicle from the Wryder Collective Featuring Worker (circa 1976).

In this story, Worker is the 19-year-old substrate of Wryder. Worker is and always has been the chore doer and the bill payer for WC. His first appearance in WC was during the sixth year of its existence and he has had virtually no periods of dormancy since that time.

Like wringin' piss out a pant leg. That's how hard it was raining, just as it had been the last 24 hours. Helluva' way for Worker to be spendin' a Saturday.

As part of a deal his buddy had gotten him into, for the last few weeks Worker had been employed by a helicopter logging outfit. They hauled trees out of the woods using big Chinook double propped helicopters with the choker rigging cables for tying on the logs hung down below them as they flew. Obviously, the logs on there too when they had a load. You needed to stay out from under their flight path, because good-sized chunks of bark and splintered wood slabs fell off continuously.

The helicopters never actually landed while they were working: loading, hauling or unloading. In the morning the aircraft would fly into a section of fallen timber, hover low, let the choker setters jump out to the ground and drop the rigging. It was the setters' responsibility to stay out of the way of the gear as it fell. The aircraft would then rise several feet and wait for the setters to choke, that is tie on, the first load or fly another team of setters or fallers, those who cut the trees down, to a different site and come back.

In the most common type of logging, two or three cables dangle from a highline, which is another heavier, overhead cable attached to a spar or heavy loader arm with a winch at one end and anchored to a solid tree or stump at the other end. The winch end typically being on the uphill and the anchor on the downhill side. The winch operator played out some line, allowing the overhead or skyline cable to go slack, it would drop down and provide enough slack in the dangling cables or chokers to allow the setters to secure them around the end of a log and lock the ball on the end of the cable to the bell further up the cable. This formed a sort of steel lasso around the log, choking tight around it when tension was applied as the overhead cable was reeled back onto the winch taking up the slack.

When the chokers are all in place, the setters scramble the hell out of the way, the lead choker man toots an electronic horn to signal to the hauler or winch operator that the logs are ready to be moved. He rolls the winch which tightens the overhead lines and lifts the logs off the ground. When they are clear of potential snags, he reels in the cable pulling the logs uphill to the landing from where they had been felled.

This is called highline logging. Worker is by no means an expert regarding this business and an experienced logger would find many flaws in his previous description, but that is basically how it works. There are variations, such as just dragging the logs out if terrain permits or grabbing them with a huge machine which cuts them off, turns the log horizontal and runs it through another cutting cycle to take off all the limbs and stacks it to wait loading onto a truck. The basic goal of getting the logs from where they are fell to where they can be loaded and hauled to a mill remains the same. The most specialized and most expensive method is helicopter logging. As with most things, the bigger and/or more powerful the machine used, the greater the expense and often the danger too.

There are unique types of choker cables used for helicopter logging. Each choker separately detaches from the main lift cable which stays attached to the aircraft. The setter would take two or three of the loose cables and tie up as many logs as he could, sometimes three or four with a single cable. Other times he may have to put two cables together to reach around one big log. Then the setters would have to drag the remaining loose ends of the chokers back to the hover zone where the Chinook would position itself for loading.   Two things were required now. First, the lead setter would have to select chokers with logs on the other end of them in such a combination that it was as close to the maximum the Chinook could lift, but not over that amount. Even if one was good at looking at irregular groups of logs and estimating weight, it was not as simple as that. Wind velocity, the shape and length of logs, how they would hang all affected drag and lift. Not every helicopter could lift the same, just like trucks some were old and tired. And most importantly, the biggest variable, the one that could initiate a fist fight at the end of the day between the lead choker man and the pilot was the fact that no two pilots ever agreed on what the maximum lift was or how bad flying conditions were. Younger pilots tended to be more cautious. Some of the older jockeys who dodged and survived flack infested LZs (landing zones) in Vietnam would try to haul just about whatever you tied on there. Then they could set the logs right on the truck instead of dumping them in a pile for a loading machine.

The second thing the lead choker man was responsible for was making sure all the loose ends of the set choker cables would reach the lift line when it was dropped from the Chinook. That meant selecting logs and assigning each one of them a choker, which were often of varying lengths, such that there would be enough slack left for the unattached ends of them all to reach the mainline cable hanging from the hovering chopper. While the lead man was accomplishing these two things he also had to be planning the next load to do the same thing as he worked his way clean across the cut zone without leaving stray logs here and there.

Hover time and time spent repositioning a helicopter was time spent burning fuel that was not moving logs and that was money. It also bit into the limited number of hours the pilots were allowed to fly each day.

The advantage of the helicopter is simple, access. They eliminate the need to build a road to the cut area and flatten out a landing for log yarding equipment, log stacking and a truck turnaround area. Note, logging companies of any size not only have a lot of log moving and hauling trucks and equipment, they also have a lot of rock and dirt hauling dump trucks, bulldozers and often a road grader for building roads.

"Regardless of what type of log extraction method is used, the loggers are legally required to clean up after themselves once an area has been cleared", Worker began to explain bucking, just before he broke into a rendition of a of a ditty he used to hear one of the bad ass, cliché fulfilling, chain sawyers sing, "I'm uh faller an' uh bucker, an' uh mean motherfucker... I don't take no shit... from no green ass twit..."

Bucking a log meant to cut it into manageable lengths if need be and cut off the limbs that would snag on stumps or other logs as it was yarded out. The limbs would also be in the way for loading and hauling the log and for processing it at the mill. Generally, in those days, the limbs were not considered to have enough value in wood to make it worth hauling them out. Today they might be used for pulp production. The limbs, bark, chunks and other scrap wood created a highly combustible debris field once it had dried out and the air got hot in late summer and early fall. This lowly, inglorious phase of the whole operation was where Worker got involved one summer.

Worker and his buddy were part of a crew of young men hired to do the cleanup. That meant gathering, piling all the limbs, chunks, etc. into about 12 separate piles from 10 to 15 feet high, depending on how far you could throw the small stuff. These were not a few un-shapely hedge trimmings or the too tall top pruned from a Christmas tree. Many of them were up to 18 inches in diameter at the butt, tapering or twisting too much to make them viable logs, but not keeping them from being heavy.

Worker and his crew mates drug what they could and piled it as high as they could, but the rest of it had to be sawn into liftable pieces. It was about a 10-acre site that needed to be cleared, piled and burned under control one pile at a time while the surrounding area was still wet enough to be insusceptible to any spark blown its way. Preventing uncontrolled fire by controlling the available fuel was the philosophy.

Again, the reason the area had been logged by helicopter was because there was no road to it and no one was going to build one either. Unlike the choker setters and fallers, Worker and the boys were not getting flown in and dropped off with their saws, fuel, lunch and whatever else they needed. No, these poor bastards were walking.

The good news was that there was a trail, of sorts. Some broken branches and an occasional orange ribbon or slash mark on a tree trunk that indicated the way the original timber cruiser who had surveyed it had traveled to get to the cutting zone. A timber cruiser is the one who marks off the area to be logged and estimates its value in terms of how many board feet of lumber it will yield. Good news pretty much ended after that.

It was 5 miles from the closest road to the cut. The chainsaws the cleanup crew used were not as large or heavy as those of the fallers, but the fuel was and neither saw nor fuel were going in through the air. These items' five-mile, uphill journey would come on the backs of Worker and the rest. Also, the splitting malls, wedges, axes, saw files, pull cables and ropes, machetes, pulaskis and the like. A guy would like a little food and water on the way in and after he got there as well.

Hmmmm, 10 miles, every day, over rough terrain, half of it before and half of it after spending 13 or 14 hours dragging heavy chunks of wood around, either going steadily uphill or knee strainingly downhill. Consideration of this fact could yield only one proposition.

Yea! A campout! So, add food, tents, cooking gear, sleeping bags, dirty magazines and any other absolute essentials needed to get through at least a week. Remember, beer ain't light either, even if it is Lite beer. "False advertising", Worker complained. With this extra category of goods now literally stacked upon the work gear, this was becoming one heavily loaded caravan.

7-8

Survival

When the loads were divvied out and balanced up as best they could be, it was decided that with three trips each they would be able to get what they needed for the first week up to the cut. Of course, on each trip they would be loaded up like the miners heading over the 3502 foot-high Chilkoot Pass on their way to the Klondike in 1898. With the others, Worker managed to get all his shit up to the site, because like them he was young, strong and stupid. Let me repeat he was stupid.

You know the old saying, "once the worst of it was over..."? There was no worst of it. It was entirely horrible for every minute. Worker stuck out the uphill death march as he would the rest of the job for several weeks, longer than most, because remember after all, he was stupid.

Once camp was set up the routine quickly and with little forethought established itself. Get up around 6 AM, throw down some pop tarts, raw toast, otherwise known as bread or lukewarm instant oatmeal. It was lukewarm because you had slept with the packet in your underwear all night, not because any attempt was made to heat any water. You just popped it in your mouth right from the bag and then added enough cold water to wash it down. After that healthy repast, Worker would join the other equally well-nourished campers and chop, saw, split, drag

7-9

Survival

and pile chunks of wood until about 7 PM. With daylight savings time in effect this left an hour or so to attempt to heat a hearty can of Dinty Moore over Sterno. Commonly, one would fortify this with a can of Spam and chase it by sucking down a warm beer.

Usually they would take a 30 to 45 min. break in the middle of the day and an occasional breather. The main purpose for these breaks was to keep from passing out and more importantly to look around, smell the fir trees and reflect on just how much one's life really sucked right now. Mostly they just worked. They were being paid by the acre cleared, not the hours worked, so peer pressure provided some motivation. Sometimes however, a perfect storm of total disinterest would form with all of them reaching the "fuck it" frame of mind simultaneously. Then, Worker and the rest of them would quit early.

Free time in the forest was not as Robin Hoodesque for Worker and the rest of the merry men as one might have hoped for. These occasions invariably and prematurely depleted the week's beer rations, so two unlucky bastards would be sent on a midweek beer run. This was not exactly like popping down to the 7 – 11 for a sixer. It was 10 miles remember, not level ones either, that you were expected to make before dark, not including the 10-

mile drive to the nearest store. The added expectation was that there was no point in even going if you didn't bring back at least five or six cases. These were the days before the aluminum can. They existed, but were still rare in comparison to the old, reliable, half pound apiece, glass, stubby. Aww the stubby, Worker remembers it with the fondness of an old friend, how it fit your hand like a mink lined mitten, except its embrace was cool and tingly rather than warm. Alas, subsequent generations are unlikely ever to be allowed the experience, the comfort, the sense of sweetness and belonging that was promised and always delivered by the embrace of the glass stubby beer bottle. Who among those whom have known the stubby will ever forget the ubiquitous, raised ring that encircled her halfway between her elegant shoulders and graceful neck? What the fuck was that for anyway, a fill line?

There was one other kind of run that was encouraged and even allowed to be made while everyone else kept working. The two doobiest looking dudes, not to be confused with dubious, though they were that too, were recruited for this mission every time and therefore exempt from the rigors of the beer run. They were of course the two most likely to come back with the medicinal miracle marijuana which made the whole fucking venture at all tolerable. To their credit, they did not disappoint, possibly motivated by the fear of death by pulaski, it's an ugly looking tool with a hoe like blade on one side, an axe blade on the opposite side and a thick wooden handle about 3 feet long.

You'd think marijuana and chainsaws would be a bad combination and you'd be right. But, Worker came out of it with all his digits and limbs. In fact, there was very little blood spillage and beer was the only transfusion they had to take intravenously. Oh yeah, if you brought back pot, you'd better bring back Goobers, Ho Hos or Oreos too. It was an otherwise staid existence they endured.

A hill or two over, three or four miles, another crew could be heard living the same existence. You could hear the chainsaw part of it anyway. Another guy on Worker's crew said that they were shit hot, worked like mules on a farm next to a dog food factory and were clearing ground like a batch of mutant agent orange, the deadly defoliant deployed in Vietnam. It was said, they were Russian.

Worker preceded Service, whom may be recalled as the key protagonist in the chronicle *Crab*, in the evolution of the set of elements eventually to become WC. Therefore, Worker did not have Service's more highly developed insight into the Cold War from which Service is a surviving veteran. A great shooting war ensued from 1914 to 1919 and flared again between 1938 and 1945. Though actually one event with an approximately 20-year hiatus from live fire, this event is typically referred to as WW I and WW II. It was at the cessation of this hot war in 1945 when the Cold War was initiated. Prior power brokers, such as Nazi Germany and England were eliminated or largely dealt out of world affairs and an ideological struggle between the eastern and western superpowers the USSR, occasionally and somewhat inaccurately referred as Russia and the USA respectively escalated.

Economic sanctions and the proliferation of world population overkill devices became the cannon fodder of confrontation rather more than mere ballistics. This had a polarizing effect resulting in a widely held belief that the other guy, be he east or west, the one opposite of you was the bad guy. The dangerous one. This was pretty much Worker's full conception of the Cold War. Although, Worker had seen the movie, *The Russians Are Coming, The Russians Are Coming!* So, his understanding of the ideological struggle had been somewhat bolstered by what he had learned from this excellent documentary. Worker was a western guy, he had never met a Russian.

One of the afternoons when the crew decided to knock off early due to the oppressive fucking heat and the

7-13

Survival

return of the Doobie Brothers, Worker declined the luxury of a clouded brain and stale beer-soaked Oreos. He headed over the hill. He could hear the saws running, no way the comrades were quitting early just because it was over 90° with ass crack welding humidity.

In an out of context remark, Worker once told me something he remembered from his campout in the cut. He still thinks of it when cued by the radio. "We've got a thing, a wave in the air, we've got a thing... Called Radar Love..." that's the cue. After one of the Doobies' returns with the substance of life, the shorter Doobie, who the fuck remembers names, started to go off on how when they had been briefly "back in the world", they had heard some Golden Earring on the radio. There was no reception in the camp. He raved and embellished on it like it had been insulin to a diabetic or crystal to a crack whore. Yeah, they were all experiencing withdrawal of some sort. The sensory deprivation was chronic and becoming acute. The meager stack of porn they'd brought was well shredded and they were ready for a new Miss Anybody, but July. So, if you're ever around Worker or Wryder as WC persona mostly goes by now and *Radar Love* starts to play, look for just a trace of mist in the corner of his tired eyes. This song was running through his brain as hiked out of camp.

7-14

Survival

It only took an hour or so before Worker was looking down on the Russians from the ridge above their clearing. He looked for something stenciled with a bear or CCCP emblazoned on it, but didn't see anything. One of the comrades looked up and waved him down, so he went on in. They were about to take a rare break, so the timing was good and they gathered up as Worker reached their camp.

After a few seconds of silence, everyone waiting for someone else to say something first, Worker said, "hello."

"Hola", came the response with a Latin accent.

"? Espanol?" asked Worker.

"Si, yo hablo Espanol."

Well, this exchange had nearly depleted the full extent of Worker's two quarters of high school Spanish, except for the big phrase he always held in reserve until he really needed it.   ?Donde esta el bano? It's good to know how to ask where the bathroom is in any language you are even remotely likely to encounter.

Nonetheless, the hike over here had been no stroll and Worker wanted to know about the Spanish speaking Russians. Fuck, this might be some kind of threat to national security. Were the Russians attempting to disguise themselves as Mexicans for God knows what reason? He pressed on gamely, but tentatively, "?Tu hables Ingleas?"

"No ?como se dice? Nada."

At one the side of the group, Worker noticed a guy starting to laugh. Worker looked his way and saw that the guy was about his own age and was now approaching.

"Hello friend, I am Nicola", the man said with either a genuine Russian accent or the best spoof of Nikita Khrushchev Worker had ever heard. Worker couldn't tell which. Both extended their hands and shook.

Through Nicola's broken and Russian accented English, Worker's ability to make inquiries in Spanish about where they crapped and varying degrees of Spanglish, Nicola, Worker and the group of about eight other guys in this camp conversed. He learned that two of them had emigrated from the Soviet Union a couple years earlier. The details did not come clear to Worker, but he got the impression they'd had to leave their families behind with little hope of ever being reunited with them.

The rest of the group were Mexican. They all had been living in Woodburn, Oregon before somehow getting together, bidding on and winning this contract. They had another one waiting for them depending on how quickly they cleared this piece.

This was serious stuff to them, they did not view it as necessarily being a temporary way of life as Worker's American sense of entitlement allowed him to see it. He saw better days ahead for sure. This group of Mexican/Russian/Americans did not break long, so the whole conversation was only about 10 minutes. Astounding what one can learn in 10 minutes. They went back to work and Worker turned back up the hill to leave their camp. He looked down as he passed by one of their heavy canvas tents, two empty vodka bottles and a full one of tequila lay on the ground. Son of a bitch!

His own camp was abuzz by the time Worker got back. More accurately, they had a buzz. Worker swallowed a can of below body temperature Dinty Moore without the use of utensils, thickened it up with a couple pieces of raw toast and went to bed.

The rest of the week played out just as the several before

had. Almost the entire crew, except Worker, their self-appointed leader and surprisingly the Doobie Brothers had turned over, that is left and been replaced. Thursday night the Doobies announced they were leaving. Worker was amazed they had lasted as long as they had, but of course they did a better job of staying detached from what was going on around them thanks to liberally inhaled dosages of the miracle substance. It was the spirit crushing, fucking boredom that got them, but the lack of even a possibility of any pussy also had to have contributed. There was some "must do" concert on Friday night and they knew they could get tickets, so Friday morning they took their mellowness, little else and headed down the hill, leaving the rest of their shit behind for the survivors to obsess over like the Donner party staring at a fresh corpse.

The crew had worked the two previous weekends and nobody was up a for third. When they knocked off early, about two that Friday afternoon they gathered in a small group and with consensus, decided to take the weekend off. This left one sticky little point however, the question that everyone was reluctant to ask. The so-called lead, finally broached it.

"Do you think we ought to leave all of our shit here with nobody in camp?"

Begrudgingly, Worker silently agreed that it was a reasonable question. There was an immediate approving chorus of guys saying, "Yeah, it'll be fine, nothing to worry about, who's gonna' bother anything". A heavy rainstorm was predicted for the weekend, anyway and that likelihood was supported by a gathering of clouds on the western horizon.

Worker knew the boys were probably right, but he also knew that people had come through here more often than one would've expected. Another group, not the Russians was working a couple of hills over in the opposite direction from Nicola and his crew. One of them had dropped in one afternoon at 4:20 and could now reasonably be expected at that time again any day. A couple of women had even gone by one day while the crew was working. Worker was pretty sure it had not been a mirage, because for a second, he caught a slight whiff of something that did not smell like fir pitch or any number of the young male excretions that permeated the air of the cut. Apparently, none of the others had seen them. Worker had been toiling off in a somewhat isolated corner of the cut. In the case that they were real, Worker had never mentioned their presence out of concern for the safety of everyone involved.

There is no point in describing what the women looked like, be they real or imagined. It didn't matter, they were women. Suffice it to say that later, after dinner and consumption of medicinals, Miss July was told by Worker to go fuck herself for the evening. She didn't seem to

7-19

Survival

mind this; the camp would refill with other receptive suitors on Monday.

At this point, I reminded Worker to get back to the whole, "leaving the shit unwatched" question. Worker agreed it would most likely be okay, 70-30 he figured. But, he also knew everyone who was automatically taking that point of view was doing so to avoid the next inevitable question sponsored by not seeing it that way. Which luckless slob would have to stay? Lead dude was visibly beginning to favor the "need to have someone watch it" side of the decision. Probably, because it obviously went against the majority and therefore presented a golden opportunity to exercise his tenuous as an ice cube on a hotplate authority.

Worker hated the prospect of going through the process of picking a method to decide who stayed, let alone the actual picking more than he hated the possibility of it being him. He could promote the seniority angle for having been in the camp longest, thereby assuring his own freedom. They could go with a short stick or lowest playing card pulled from a deck lottery. Ask for a volunteer, yeah. The things boys with boners volunteer for is a pretty specific, small set of activities and does not include two days in a rainstorm, in a tent, not alone anyway. The leader guy with his approval rating equal to

Hitler's amongst the Jews, could just appoint someone. Worker considered that one and almost suggested it just to see who survived.

For the last couple of weeks Worker had been sliding further into that "Aw fuck it" emotional pit and frame of mind wherein current circumstances didn't matter, regardless of what they were. A sign of too much magic potion, he assayed. 4:20 had been coming more often every day. Worker didn't much relish a five-mile slog through the soon to be upon them rain, either. The trail would be slick and muddy. He could be wet and cold and as sick of shit as well here as he could anywhere else. So, before everyone began to Clarence Darrow their own case as to who would be picked to stay, Worker said, "I'll stay. You guys go and I'll see ya' all Monday morning." At the time, it seemed reasonable.

45 minutes later, Worker was the king of a tent city ghost town that was getting pissed all over like God had just finished a three-pitcher pizza. He noted the wind, which wasn't too bad. Strong winds tended to bring down limbs, dead men as they were called and it was best to be mindful of where one stood or what one walked under when the air started to move.

7-21

Survival

Worker headed for his tent. He got there, crawled into it, ate a couple pieces of raw toast with a pad of cold butter in the middle of it that wouldn't spread any easier than the legs of an Amish virgin and finished a couple pieces of jerky that a mouse had started on after gnawing his way into the sealed tight bag. It was designed to keep freshness in, but not mice out. Two conditions Worker judged to be mutually exclusive as he almost tasted the jerky before swallowing it.

There are couple of things it is good to be when you or your world are miserable. One is high. The other is so freaking tired neither miserable nor high matters. Worker had the latter going for him, he relaxed to the point of liquification and poured himself into his sleeping bag. In his sleep, the two women who walked past the cut earlier stopped and so did the rain.

That was a dream which ended about 1 AM when Worker felt cold water flowing through the crack of his ass and rising. He clicked on his flashlight and assessed his situation. If misery loves company, it was shit outta' luck this time as the women had only been part of the dream. Unreal, just like the thought about the rain having stopped.

7-22

Survival

In the dim yellow glow of failing battery flashlight illumination minor salvation rose above the growing torrent. Water was now starting to lap at his scrotum, not in the good way and to float discarded Dinty Moore labels to the downstream side of the tent. Why he'd saved the labels Worker couldn't remember now. Maybe he'd planned on helping Dinty hook up with Miss July. A wet ass and a clear memory apparently being mutually exclusive in Worker's case.

His buddy, the one who originally hooked them up with this gig of the damned had had the common sense to bail out for good a couple of weeks earlier. When he'd left he had not announced it would be permanent, but a few days later Worker got a note from him sent up via the Doobie Brothers, saying he wouldn't be back and asking Worker to bring his shit out for him when he eventually rejoined the living.

Galling at the time, but fortuitous at this moment. His sleeping bag was still there. It was over on the dry side of the tent, which was elevated several inches above Worker's own nest. It was damp, but everything always was in weather like this. The air was as humid as a jungle,

lacking only the equatorial heat to make it unbearable.

Survival

The other bag felt like the Sahara after Worker had shucked his wet clothes and slid into it. Small comfort this in any other moment, a nod from God that night. Worker let the last few electrical embers from his flashlight burn out, but he "... *Raged against the dying of the light...*"[9], as they spilled their last few photons.

Morning and the dawn of a new day changed Worker's outlook on his present situation. It made it worse with nothing, but even bleaker outcomes foreshadowed. The monsoonal shower was unabated, had intensified if possible and the sky was dimmer than his flashlight had been during its last seconds of unspent voltage. Yeah, this was much worse. He'd slept well after his water polo match. The downside to that being that now he would not be able to sleep the whole day away. Sleep is a pretty good way to pass time which would be much more uncomfortably spent if one were conscious. He cursed himself for not being one of those prison lifers who had through years of diligence trained themselves to sleep 22 or 23 hours a day while in solitary confinement.

Seemed he just couldn't catch a break. There are ways other than sleep to affect consciousness, however and Worker was beginning to form a plan. Well, a desire at

---

[9] Dylan Thomas

least. The difference between a plan and a desire being at times dramatic. For example, a small boy may say he wants to be a gynecologist (or a fireman) when he grows up. That his is plan, similar in scope to Worker's current thinking. A young man explains how he will get into a good college, major in premed, go to med school at Johns Hopkins, intern, etc. He has a plan.

Worker would come up with one too, but first he needed sustenance. The soggy shit floating away from his own campsite was still catchable, but he figured he could do better and he had the whole place to rummage through. That would kill a little time too. Worker donned his raingear, cinched it tight enough for a spacewalk and trekked towards the tent farthest from his. No use in pissing off the neighbors when he could take advantage of the folks on the wrong, wrong only because it was on the opposite side of the cut.

The first one he came to was an army surplus pup tent. He didn't even bother, both the flaps had been left open, presumably to let it air out. Water was rushing through it now and it was serving more as a storm culvert than as a shelter.

A slight aside here to clear up one point you more experienced woodsmen and campers may be wondering about. Why wasn't the food store hanging from a tree to protect it and anyone near it from wildlife such as bears or a cougar? According to Worker, these guys were stupid and/or tired and/or high to the point of not giving a shit most of the time. Also, Worker noted, between the chainsaw noise 14 hours a day, the fire at night, and the constant stench of blood, sweat and sticky underwear emanating from camp like a deadly mushroom cloud, no bear his right mind or with functional olfactory senses was coming anywhere near the place. Cougars, well if they want something, they're gonna' get it no matter how high you hang it and if they want to hurt you, they will. Then of course, there is always that protective umbrella of good luck that God seems to extend over any true dumbass.

Okay, that cleared up, so, uh, yeah, Worker whiffed in both senses of the word at the first tent. The next one offered signs of being a winner as he saw scattered pastry wrappers drifting around it. Eureka! Just inside the flap was an unopened one dozen pastry pack. He lifted it. It did not feel right, too heavy, waterlogged. There, on the corner of the wrapping were tiny tooth marks indicating where a mouse had breached the protective plastic packaging, the barrier that normally gives these things a shelf life of about 14 years. These things had soaked up water like an octogenarian does wrinkle cream. "Fuck!" thought Worker, "nobody likes a soggy Sara Lee."

Bears and cougars are one thing. There really isn't any defense against rodents.

Worker wasn't completely discouraged yet, but prospects had bleakened. Ahoy! What's this, just off the port bow of the "SS, You're Fucked Pal", Worker imagined himself to be navigating. Aye! (Okay, enough pirate crap, sorry, Worker does that sometimes.) Worker was at the Doobie Brothers' tent. On the one hand, you couldn't expect those blazoids to have left as much as a mouth sized morsel. On the other hand, they were pretty fucked up when they left, so who knows what they may have forgotten. Fuck it! Worker was the soggy definition of a man with nothing to lose by checking it out.

He approached the tent through a debris field one might have expected to find had there been a Hostess Twinkies factory right next to Chernobyl. They had all been living like animals for weeks, but "Mother Teresa on a unicycle", these fuckers were primordial, pre-Cambrian. Worker was sure the history of evolution on this planet would repeat itself if this environment he now entered was left undisturbed long enough.

Worker had no desire to see that happen, so he started searching through the anthropological ruins by kicking it apart with his foot. He nudged one hill apart and he saw a flash of something golden or brown, but an empty can rolled back in place to obscure it again. The thought of sticking his hand in there froze him with trepidation, but he had a pair of wet leather gloves in his pocket. He slipped the left one on. Worker was right-handed, but why risk the party hand, he figured? Son of a bitch! A package, unopened, dry, no tooth marks, and entire package of Lorna Doones. He'd always loved that bitch! A little more excavation yielded a banana moon pie, some barely nibbled on jerky, two Ding Dongs still in their foil, a bag of unopened, but crushed and powderized Funyuns, and the ubiquitous odd edibles. Worker may have been preparing his Last Supper, but it was gonna' be a buffet.

Just as he had plundered all that he thought he could and was about to leave, Worker noticed one of those plastic, watertight first aid kits jammed into a corner of the tent. Why not, might be some aspirin in there and he was pretty sure he would be needing it later. As worker opened the case he was engulfed by a celestial blue glow emanating from its interior. The wider he pulled open the lid, the more the azure illumination brightened until all the inside of the tent glowed in soft neon like being

Survival

backlit by a Hamm's Beer sign on a foggy night through a cloud of volcanic ash[10].

The Doobies, God bless those spaced out bastards, had left the magic behind. No papers, but those would get wet anyway and there was a $.99 corncob pipe tucked in the first aid kit next to a snake bite treatment packet. This was far and away the best equipped first aid kit Worker had ever seen. There was even a Band-Aid or two in it.

Booty in hand, Worker trudged and sloshed towards his own tent. He felt much better about his immediate prospects, but something still nagged at the back of his mind. It was like he'd forgotten something or perhaps things weren't going to go exactly as he planned.

He dove into his tent, rustled through his backpack, the one with the new, irregularly shaped hole coincidentally located in the pocket where he stored his matches. He did not recall having seen that hole before. Worker extracted the plastic bag the matches had been stored in, the bag with that new, irregularly shaped hole in it perfectly congruent to the hole in the pack pocket. The matches were damp. Fucking mice!

---

[10] Another Chronicle for another time.

Worker tried to strike one of the matches. The white, head part of it sloughed off like powdered sugar. He struck another with a little less pressure, same result. The next one he dragged slowly across the surface of an inexplicably dry piece of bark he found. The sulfurous igniter tip of the match disintegrated more slowly, but still dissipated into powder without the hint of a spark. He'd seen the cheap, disposable Bic lighters that were just beginning to be marketed, but had thought being so cheap meant they weren't worth having. There was that never passing cloud of stupid again.

Worker had a few books of paper matches scattered throughout his pack and he dug them out and tried them all. Fucking moisture! Fucking mice!

Re-donning his rain jacket, Worker braved the monsoonal squall once again, though truth be told, it was only slightly wetter outside of the tent than in it. Under heavy clouds of both rain and stupid, Worker cursed himself for not having thought of matches on his first pillaging rampage through the canvas and nylon hamlet.

He hadn't been looking for them specifically, still he did not recall having seen any matches or one of those now not so worthless, "cheap" lighters in any of the tents he had already ransacked. So, he started towards the abodes

Survival

he had not previously plundered. The search began in earnest. It was like trying to find one of your own kind and own gender on Noah's Ark. He found nary a match that wasn't wet as a clam's ass at high tide.

Now, like most of you, Worker knew that theoretically one could start a fire by rubbing two sticks together. They always tell you that in any kind of survival story. What they don't say is that this only works if one of the sticks is a match. A dry match. Now, if you're an Aborigine in the outback of Australia where everything around you is drier than a popcorn fart and ready to spontaneously combust, then you had a pretty good chance. Hell, if you aren't careful you could ignite your own pubic hair just by rubbing your legs together in the Outback. Not so much in the Northwest during a downpour so hard the rain was bouncing back up at you from the ground in case it had missed you on the way down.

He stood outside the last unsearched tent, Worker had one last chance to pilfer successfully, so he unzipped the flap and stepped into it. He had evaluated it as a good sign that the flap had been closed tight and that the tent was high enough to stand up in. He stepped in and was now standing in 5 to 6 inches of water amidst a flotilla of drifting food staples and candy wrapper flotsam. All packs and bags of any sort were tipped over laying horizontal

7-31

Survival

and the scene looked vaguely like the Bismarck after its encounter with the HMS Hood. Then a greenish, plastic, square object bobbed to the surface, apparently having broken loose from its anchorage under the edge of a soaked sleeping sack that Worker had jostled with his foot. It had a switch on it, one of those pushbutton types covered with the thin white rubber switch condom to seal out moisture. The lens was intact and not foggy inside from moisture either. This was one of those big flashlights that used the old, two pounds worth of six-volt dry cell battery with both the plus and minus poles on the same end, the top. Each pole was a conductive coil which stayed in contact, one with the bulb and one with the bulb housing, because of the spring tension from the coils. Worker pushed the switch in and the light and came on. He pondered, "this could be something."

At the very least, it never hurt to have a functional, waterproof to boot flashlight. He took the light and slogged for home shit home! The rest of the idea that had begun to formulate when he first saw the flashlight was near fully percolated by the time Worker backstroked into his own tent.

Worker snatched up a couple of the damp headed wooden matches he hadn't yet ruined. Next, he shuffled back through his pack pockets and found the third

7-32

Survival

element he would need to animate his personal *Quest for Fire* (great movie).

Like every other ferrous material in this part of the country, the steel wool part of the SOS pad he gleaned from his disorganized crap was beginning to rust and most of the blue soap stuff had flaked off it. It didn't matter. He wasn't planning on cleaning anything and it wasn't so rusty that it wouldn't still conduct a little low voltage, low amperage, direct current electricity. Worker had an old kerosene lantern as well, so he braced that upright, propped up the glass chimney and felt to make sure the wick was saturated with fuel. This would be the protective vessel, the carrying chamber. Worker was not yet sure if or how many times he would be able to make fire. But, if the gods of the saturated whose providence he now understood he was under did grant him glorious combustion, he would protect that red yellow gleaming flame like it was The Virgin Mary's own maidenhead.

The End.

"Oh, fuck you Worker! Get on with the rest of the story, so I can finish writing this shit down!" I barked at him.

He replied, "Well, it's kind of anti-climactic from here on out."

"Finish the God damn story, these people can't fall any further to sleep anyhow."

"Well, okay."

Worker unscrewed the lens ring from the flashlight, pulled it apart and took out the chunky battery. He sturdied it between his feet, grasp a couple of the unstrikeable matches with his left hand and the disintegrating SOS pad in the right. Worker arced the SOS pad by touching it to both battery poles simultaneously and sure as shit, sparks flew out of it. Worker moved the matches into position to catch a few of the randomly popping sparks. When a spark hit them, the matches ignited, and their heads blazed. Absorbed in self-admiration, Worker allowed the matches to burn down to the wooden shafts before he moved to ignite the lantern.

The lantern wick caught instantly, Worker adjusted the flame to low, so it would not heat up the damp and cold glass chimney too quickly and cause it to break. He warmed his hands around the tiny flame, while protecting it from any errant and evil intentioned breeze until he was able to lower the chimney into place. Worker gradually adjusted the flame higher by twisting the knob ended rod that withdrew and extended the length of wick exposed to the air, hence the height of the flame.

"It was motherfuckin' glorious!" Worker exalted.

"You swear too much." I said to Worker. "There's no need for that. You're semi-articulate, at least enough to just tell what happened. You don't need to throw all of that in their just for effect, shock, realism, or whatever you're going for."

"Eat shit fuckstick", was his reply. "I ain't goin' for any effect. I'm just tellin' ya' how it was an' how I felt about it at the time. I don't care if you're an Outback wanderin' asshole from "Dingo Pissed Here Creek", Australia or Neil Armstrong firin' up the LEM to get the fuck offa' the moon; there are moments when making fire is more satisfying than poppin' Margaret Thatcher's cherry, you know, when she was younger, before she became the Iron Lady. When you're wet, cold and pissed off at the world, because you're wet and cold and that is startin' to look like a permanent condition... Well, fire ain't just kinda' cool, it isn't nice, rather fortuitous, or a pleasant outcome to one's efforts. It's Fuckin' Glorious!"

"Do you get that now shithead?" he continued. "Making fire, when you need to, in an unconventional, let alone in a way you never thought of before, that's survival! That was being a man in the mid-20th century for all those male baby boom bastards who were too late to tough it out West in a covered wagon and were never going to win a world war. Learning to control fire is the most important survival skill ever learned by an erect walking hominid. Like a first period validates womanhood; making fire, a rampaging, chemical reaction of rapid oxidation from previously static elements always has and always will validate manhood.

Descartes's Cenozoic doppelgänger probably said, "I make fire; therefore, I am man!" Next, he kicked back and inhaled the smoke from it, as would Worker.

He had fire stored now and could even make it again if he had to. There was plenty of fuel in the lantern and more if he needed it. He could build a fire outside if the rain ever let up. If not, he'd fire up a can of Sterno, put it under the grill on his little folding Sterno burner and raise the temperature of a wet can of something, now ill-legibly labeled, to about 5° above ambient. It could be Dinty, it could be peaches, fuck it, in a few minutes it wouldn't matter if it was a can of Alpo. In a few minutes, Alpo would probably be looking fucking tasty. There was the Sterno stove and a mystery can on his left. The first aid kit, the most excellent one, was on his right.

All the elements of WC share a common trait. They travel the middle-of-the-road as long as possible, delaying every decision to be made with the hope that it will eventually just go away. It does so more often than all of those fucked up, proactive, would be managers of the world will ever admit. That would be like a magician revealing how all his tricks are done. Then what would he do for a living? WC has found that the natural resolution, even if it is dissolution is usually the best solution. Even when it isn't, it's still the easiest one to come up with. No energy is spent on it; therefore, one remains rested to clean up the shit on those rare occasions when the action of no action goes awry resulting in an undesirable outcome.

For Worker, this was not one of those times. The choice here was a clear-un. If one were about to consume both marijuana and ambient +5° Alpo within the immediate future, which do you think ought to be consumed first? (Aside: By the Way, Alpo is a fucking metaphor, so quit asking why it was carried uphill 5 miles. If you must take it literally, well then, okay, they were trying to make a pet out of a coyote.) A rare easy decision for Worker and WC.

Worker packed that corncob bowl to a perfectly flammable density. He used a little twist of toilet paper from a roll he had taken great pains to keep dry as a match to transfer the vindication of manhood from the lantern to the bowl. Like a piece of soft sandstone in a lapidariest's rock tumbler, the edges soon came off his reality.

The Alpo turned out to be succotash and suck it he did. Straight from the can of course, but between noisy, guttural slurps he reheated the can to just above not cold, over the flickering Sterno can.

Sterno Digression

For the benefit of any younger and most likely more urban readers than Worker, let me explain what Sterno is. Or was, as I do not know if it is still available. It may be, but if so it's intended use is probably more aesthetic only these days. Keeping hot dishes warm on the table by flame, lending dinner more of a "candlelight" aspect, for example. Its origins I believe are in the 1930s, maybe earlier, maybe later as part of the flood of gimmickry incubated by the 1940s war effort. Simply, it is a can of fuel for flame. Like a candle, but it burns longer, at a more consistent temperature and is more resistant to being blown out by a gust of air. It is pink in color, has a waxy texture when cool. It liquefies and then vaporizes as it heats and burns. It comes in a can resembling a tuna fish can in shape, but slightly larger. Sterno's function is to heat a pan of something. The most popular employment of it was to heat a baby bottle of milk in a pan of water in the days before rural electrification or the widespread advent of gas burners. Instead of building a fire in the cook stove in the middle of the night or when it was already 100° inside and out, one could just pop the lid off a can of Sterno, light it, and then set the lid back over the can when ready to extinguish it. Of course, it went out of use with the popularization of modern ranges and microwaves. It made a small market for itself as a camp and backpacking fuel. You could buy a lightweight, aluminum folding device that held the can and had a small grill above it to set a pan on. This was Worker's set up. Lightweight white gas, butane and propane camp stoves soon replaced it, however. So, if it is still around it is probably confined to a small niche in the romantic or elegant dinner market.

Own World, Own Rules

Worker did not allow the corncob to cool very long that evening as he depleted the first aid kit. He also partook greedily, glutinously and slovenly (most of the seven sins popped up sometime that night) from his earlier plunder. The fact that it had been willfully taken, literally harvested from another man's larder, stolen if you will, just made it taste all the better. That and the pot, of course. He had no neighbors, so obviously no neighbor's

7-39

Survival

wife, but between bowls and bitefulls he openly coveted Miss August in fulfillment of one more sin. He could have Miss July any time he wanted, in fact had done so for several weeks. He had stayed true to her out of some sort of perverted loyalty vow. It was as if he was trying to stay attached to the real world somehow by clinging to its rules and mores even though there was no way they could be applied to this shithole. But no more, not that night, he wanted some strange and by God, he'd have it. He'd take it just as he had the rest of that night's bounty.

Miss August succumbed to his will several times that night, vindicating his manhood over and over, but never so much as did the little flame in the lantern that illuminated his last night of self-debauchery in the cut.

Costco

A Motorcycle Chronicle from the Wryder Collective Featuring Oryder (circa 2007).

In this story, Oryder, the fiftyish, gravity-challenged, (plump) yet reasonably-capable-appearing substrate element of WC encounters WC's longest enduring challenge; he tries to avoid becoming a public spectacle.

There is no limit to the number of places a capably appearing, albeit fat man in shorts can be humiliated on a hot, sweaty day. Costco is as good as any. This is a destination Oryder had come to loathe and one he would not have been found at had the sudden need for a fifty-five-gallon drum of barbecue sauce and a forty-eight-roll pack of ass-wipe tissue plus sundries not become imperative. When one needs the staples, one goes to Costco.

Truth be told, all elements of WC have endured an almost obsessive trepidation regarding embarrassment since the inception of the collective set, WC, to which they all belong and permutate within to construe the Wryder Persona. Disconcertion, embarrassment, frustration mere discomfort, quantify it how you will; it is nonetheless disquieting to one's self esteem when one becomes one of the very objects for which one has always held considerable disdain. Oryder, for as long can be remembered has held a high degree of disgust for those people in the checkout line at any store who still pay by writing a check. C'mon, that went out with the Commodore 64 and the last functioning typewriter! The disgust is compounded directly by the length of the line behind the check writer and particularly one's position in that line.

A number of questions roll ceaselessly over in the mind, "My God, how many more of these check writing citizens of Bedrock can still be ahead of me!? No! It can't be all of them, can it!?" How often that has come out aloud one is not sure, but the brain is certainly screaming, "c'mon, c'mon, swipe a fucking credit card, debit card, do a retinal scan, what the fuck ever and let's all get back to the world of the living!"

On this particular day at Costco, Oryder handled his shallow percolating emotion without an outward appearance of frustration, whilst a woman with a purse the size of Popeye's sea bag waited until every item she had on her three flatbed industrial dollies, two self-propelled, articulating carts of items and the one-hundred and eighteen-inch TV she had produced a merchandise slip for at the last moment was delivered to the register and everything had been rung up by the clerk. After confirming the grand total three times she asked the clerk to recalculate it, even though she had checked to see that all of the inputs for each individual item were correct. This apparently, "just in case", the barcode scanner with the acuity of an electron microscope or the electronic register with one-hundred-thousand times more computing power than had been available for the last moon landing, "had made a mistake".

Then and only then did she hoist her duffel up onto the counter and go on an armpit deep scavenger hunt for a checkbook which invariably had no pen attached to it, hence necessitating another Cousteauian deep dive back into the "Santa's-endless-bag-o'-toys-size" ruck.

But what can one do? One can't kill them. That might be considered an overreaction in some quarters. One sucks it up, bites the lip and swallows the aggression along with all of the other shit sandwiches life thoughtfully continues to prepare for one. There are other greater or equally as egregious checkout line actions: the last minute "change of mind", when suddenly a quantity of two instead of one or a different brand or size of an object is impulsively required. Also, the rare, but exacerbating negative response to the ubiquities, "did you find everything you need?" question. That's just something they have to say – the answer is always yes, yes dammit yes – do not send them searching for something now. Consider too the "oh I had a coupon" surprise announcement that always, just follows the otherwise completed transaction. Once in a while, there will be a question that makes you wonder why they are still walking around, such as, "Have you seen my son?" To summarize, Oryder despises anyone who holds up the checkout line that he is in, but he can't kill them.

Oryder, now with beard, finally made it to the front of the checkout line, handed the clerk his American Express Card or Visa or whatever the only one they were currently accepting was. She rang up his total and asked, "On the card?"

"Sure", he replied, she didn't think he was gonna' write a check, did she?

"Sir, this card is expired", she informed him.

What the fuck! That'd never happened to him before. He had to verify the date on the card himself, the card he only used at COSTCO, the placed he had successfully been able to avoid coming to for a long time. Son of bitch! It had expired. He had less than three dollars cash on him. "You don't take any other cards do you?" he asked, already knowing the answer.

She confirmed this, but added, "You can pay with any debit card if you have one". The slightly more evolved cousin to the check, hell no he didn't have any. Oryder was a credit card or cash man, tried and true and just a little too far into the old fart stage of life to be changin' now, still more evolved than the check writer, however. The irony was lost on him at the time.

Too bad he didn't have a chicken-feed-sack sized purse to dive into. That would have given his mind a few seconds to clear. He had become that which he despised, the asshole at the front of the line stealing

COSTCO 4

minutes from the lives of all those people behind him who were able to pay their own way through life and COSTCO.

From the corner of his eye and then directly as he glanced to his left, he saw a cash machine about ten yards away. There's the ticket, so he says to the clerk, "If you give me a minute I can pay cash", head gesturing towards the cash vendor as he spoke.

"Sure", she said, "we can give you a minute".

Oryder heard her reply, the relaxed and soothing tone of it anyway, so, casually, slowly even, he meandered towards the automated teller, somewhat smug in having turned that situation around so quickly without having become the ire of disgust for all those behind him in line.

He got to the cash machine, eased out his wallet, thumbed reflectively through a few cards, selected the one he wanted, wiped the back of it on his shirt to remove any wallet residue from the magnetic strip, paused several seconds to recall his pin number and wondered just how much money he had in his account. He knew there was enough, but still wanted to know where he stood balance wise.

The pin number finally came to Oryder as he mumble-sang the little ditty he used as a mnemonic device for the code. He slid the card in, picked English, waited for the menu screen to come up and unhurriedly selected account inquiry, checking and savings please. Yes, he would like a printout of the transaction. The machine hesitated a moment and then whirred and spit out the ink on paper version of his business. Hey! More in there than he thought, sweet!

"Would you like another transaction?" the screen blinked.

"Certainly," he confirmed by pushing the yes button. "Let's have some of that cash, and, uh, better print it out again." The machine discharged another receipt and some $20 bills, four of the five would be required, so he slipped only one of them into his wallet.

He turned back towards the register. It wasn't a firing squad, but everyone in the line he had come from was shooting him the same "sometime today ass hole!" look.

Oh, "*we'll* wait for you", that's what the clerk had said. Oryder heard and understood the "*we*" part of her remark now. He had unhurriedly meandered to and malingered at the cash machine thinking she would push his stuff to the side and checkout the next person or two in line while he retrieved some green.

Oryder's unpaid for merchandise still lay sprawled across the checkout stand conveyor top like drift wood on a hurricane swept beach. The clerk and packer had decided not to box it until they were sure it was going to be paid for.

All eyes were on him, as if he were a rodeo clown just after the bull had thrown the cowboy. They wanted some quick action. He paid the $79 and a few cents tally, threw his stuff in the cart, put his change in his pocket and started rolling for the door.

It'd been a little embarrassing, but he'd been a jackass before. Long day, mostly over, forget it he figured. Go home, it'd be funny later.

About halfway to the exit where the door monitor magic-markers a line through the receipt, just as Oryder was passing the hot dog or Polish line, he looked down and saw a quarter in front of his left foot. Lesser change, eh, forget it, but it's hard to forget what one could've done with the quarter as a kid. Candy out the kazoo. Now, a quarter only buys one eighth of a vending machine Coke. But old habits die hard, a synapse of boyish glee fired in his brain, so he stopped, stooped his fat ass over and picked it up.

He dropped it into his pocket. But, hey! Wait! There was another quarter, couple of dimes, a nickel and a some of pennies on the ground. Oryder thought he felt something roll down his leg as he sucked in his gut, preparing to stoop again and make his next grab. Then he saw the "second" quarter he was grabbing was the same original Virginia State Coin he had just retrieved. Suddenly, he remembered the hole in the front left-hand pocket of these denim shorts he was wearing.

Forced out of his normal habit by this hole, Oryder had been dropping his change in the other pocket with his keys since he had begun wearing these pants. Any man alive will tell you this just does not feel natural. It takes a fair amount of conscious effort to suppress the nearly auto-functional habit of dropping one's change into a pocket other than the one where it usually goes.

This level of concentration had not been induced or rather had been suppressed due to the pressure he had succumbed to while being the jackass/spectacle holding up the checkout line and having to use all available mental facilities to suppress the flight instinct. Finally, being allowed to give lease to this instinctual drive, one does so with no thought to ancillary tasks, such as where change should go. So, the mundane, more routine function operates unconsciously under stress, reverting to habits controlled mainly by the subconscious or entirely auto-reflexively. Oryder had dropped his change into his left-hand pocket and precipitated his escape from the checkout stand as quickly as he could.

Psychobabble aside, he picked up Virginia again and snagged the dimes too, stood up and looked back down at the pennies and the nickel then reflexively decided, screw it! He wasn't bending his fat ass over again, for seven cents. There was little doubt in his mind that the way his luck was running at the moment, either the ass would rip out of his pants which sweat had adhered to his butt cheeks, or the strain of bending over his gut would unleash a rumbling, attention attracting fart or both. Oryder figured he'd had all he wanted of the limelight. Besides, the magic-marker man was beckoning for his receipt and people were beginning to bunch up behind him with receipts in their hands and "not you again asshole" looks in their eyes. The would-be Costco refugee turned to flee.

"Mr. Hey Mr. you dropped your money", came a sweetly, high pitched voice of charity and good will. It belonged to one of two angelic looking little old ladies giving up their place in the hot dog or Polish line to come to Oryder's aid.

As she called to Oryder, just loud enough to turn every set of eyes in a twenty-foot radius on him, she flashed a sweet little old lady smile.

He knew what was coming. Fuck! Did he ever want to knock her out!?

"We'll help you Mr."

He tried to protest by saying, "Oh no, it's okay, don't bother." Of course, it was too late, they'd already sprang into action. He suspected sweet little old ladies, like these two, had probably been kind their whole lives, had been good mothers and grandmothers, and... lived for these kinds of moments. Yeah, me too... he grimaced.

The one with the voice rebuffed his protestation with the most imaginably melodic, "Oh, no, will get them for you, no one has enough money with the way things are today."

Shit! When would this end? One more act of kindness directed towards him would probably send him over the edge.

Ah! Twice a spectacle in the last 5 minutes. There stands the fat, but otherwise normally-healthy-appearing bastard leaning casually on a shopping cart while two sweet, shriveled octogenarians overtaxed their blood pressure medication, stooped over rounding up his pennies. Yeah, this is the image one likes to put on public display.

With surprising agility, the voiceless woman came up with the nickel and a penny cleanly on her first pass and handed them to him with only a smile. He thanked her, the least a fat, lazy bastard could do; he had no doubt. The gallery of those just out of the checkout line and heading for the door or waiting to buy a hot dog or Polish had fixed their gaze on him at this point. "Come on, there are plenty of other directions which you could point your eyes in", Oryder pleaded internally.

He was still standing there, a chunky, slovenly spectacle of modern American manhood. The voice lady made an initial, but unsuccessful grab at the remaining penny. You could hear the increased labor in her breathing as well as the crackling in her knees as she remained hunched over, posing for another try. Strike two!

Fuck! She is of a generation that does not give up.

Christ! Oryder pondered, "if she goes down, should I jump to her aid or just get out of the way of the encroaching villagers with their pitchforks and torches?"

One more grab, it didn't look good, she'd found the range and was in position, but couldn't quite get those knuckle-swollen, arthritic, fingers too close around Mr. Lincoln. With a final gasp just short of a death rattle, she dropped a little lower and scooped in the Great Emancipator with an awkward, but effective two-handed method. She straightened up accompanied by the theme song from a bowl of Rice Krispies and a face as reflectively white as the Cliffs of Dover.

"Here you are sir", sweet as honey-battered fudge, "here's your money... dear". Oryder wasn't sure of the whole quote verbatim, except for the "dear" part. He knew he'd heard that.

He thanked her profusely and smiled at her as sincerely as he could with stares all around him insinuating he was a steaming dog turd in the sandbox someone's child had just crawled out of.

Oryder turned, slinked to the magic-marker-man, made it to his car in 1.5 seconds, evaporated out of the Costco parking lot and relished the hellish traffic jam he was now anonymously part of. He considered the roll he was on and carefully repositioned his hands so they were nowhere near the horn button on his steering wheel.

About the Author

The author of this book went back to college after serving in the armed forces for several years, becoming the first in his family to complete a four-year degree. He worked briefly as a teacher and counselor, but did not find that to be his calling.

He is now a retired blue-collar worker, having spent more than thirty years sweating and occasionally straining at the manufacture or manipulation of one machine or another.

Robert has always wanted to be a writer and sporadically through the years of physical toil has taken time to put words onto paper. However, his self-assessment was that he was not naturally born to the task of composition.

An author who was both cousin and friend, Jim McChesney, concurred with this evaluation during one of their conversations, but offered the following. "Bob", Jim told him, "you are a genetically predetermined, dyed in the wool storyteller."

Taking this to heart and with time now available to him, Robert has "written" down a few stories. Author or not, close enough to bother arguing about, he figures.

90062777R00115

Made in the USA
Columbia, SC
25 February 2018